As It Seemed To Me

An account of the highs, lows, accomplishments and failures as a Labour Party official, Trade Union Officer, musician and photographer - and the good and not so good people who were part of it all

Phil Graham

If after reading this you still want me to dinner, I'll be happy to come.

Phil

FILMAR Publications

23 Park View Terrace, New Coundon
BISHOP AUCKLAND, Co.Durham, DL14 8QB

Dedicated to the life and memory of
Mike Findley MBE
a dear friend and true inspiration

February 14th 1945 – June 15th 2019

Note and explanation...

Ever since the publication in November 2015 of my book, I'm Going Nowhere! the success of which continues to raise funds for the charity GAIN (Guillain-Barre & Associated Inflammatory Neuropathies) a number of readers along with my wife Janet, have suggested that I write another. It is most flattering, of course, but as I wrote in the preface at the time I am not a professional writer and I do not believe I have anything further to offer which could be of interest to others. My life and experiences will be of little consequence except perhaps to a limited number of family members. Likewise, my accomplishments, mainly music, photography, trade unionism and politics, will have scant appeal beyond others who are similarly inclined. Moreover, I have set myself firmly against those kind souls who champion the *just write anything'* cause. The thought of developing fictional characters and situations is anathema and best left to those who have a natural ability in that regard.

Nevertheless, the flattering onslaught continued, triggered, I suppose, by the hugely successful launch of I'm Going Nowhere! where more than one hundred friends, strangers, members of the press, health professionals and family piled into The Park Head Hotel in New Coundon to witness the event. The book was an instant success, albeit to a limited readership at that point in time: a readership, incidentally, which later grew to include those around the country who had GBS or who knew someone with the illness. A number of books were sold to readers in Canada, South Africa and the USA respectively.

Janet brought her well honed organisational skills into play ensuring the launch was well publicised and the hotel owners, Tony & Claire Gibbons, for whom Janet works as duty manager, generously granted us free use of their main function room and laying on a sumptuous post-launch buffet. I remain, therefore, ever grateful to them. Our esteemed guest speakers were key to what we were trying to achieve; to promote the book in order to raise funds for GAIN. Neurology Consultant, Neil Archibald from James Cook University Hospital explained graphically, yet in layman's terms, what GBS is and how it affects those who are stricken. Caroline Morris from GAIN head office in Lincolnshire, followed with an engaging outline of the aims and purpose of the charity.

I signed and sold one hundred and twelve books that day, cheerfully acquiescing that the launch had exceeded my wildest expectations. The subsequent report and photo coverage in our regional newspaper, The Northern Echo, led to a series of radio interviews with BBC Tees, Radio Teesdale and Bishop FM Radio each in turn leading to further book sales.

So, I gave up, threw in the towel and capitulated, agreeing to once again put pen to paper, or rather fingers to the keyboard to try and make an account of my life in music, photography, the Communication Workers Union and The Labour Party worthy of reading. Should readers continue beyond this point they will judge whether I and my flattering persuaders are right or wrong.

By way of further validation it is said that most of us have memories of our grandparents and, in some instances, our great grandparents. But who can say they have memories of great, great grandparents and beyond? Fundamentally then, this work is legacy vanity providing an accessible record for future generations of Grahams by describing events which have been a major part of my life.

During my teenage years and on into my twenties I concealed confused thoughts about the world, society, communities and people; thoughts which I could not adequately articulate. Neither overtly left wing nor right wing throughout those early years, there was nonetheless a growing and compelling awareness of the impact that governments and officialdom have on our lives. Such impact became distinct in the early nineteen seventies when watching black and white television news footage of Irish men, women and children in their 'struggles' against the British army and those who were not of their own religious and political persuasion. Images of burning buildings and cars in Derry and Belfast bore into my senses. The television images were one thing but the human misery, bigotry and sacrifice behind what I was seeing was on a much higher scale in terms of the emotional intensity and sense of helplessness stirring inside me. And yet I was both alarmed and intrigued in equal measure. More so because of my proud paternal lineage to that tortured province. Years later, visiting relatives, I fell in love with the rebuilt and flourishing Belfast and with the delightful, almost timeless towns of Ballynure and Ballyclare where my father grew up prior to settling in England as a teenager after the second world war.

All of this was taking place not long after I had been given my first guitar. In August 1967, the so called summer of love, I had just turned fourteen and was on holiday in northern Italy with my mother and brother, Andy. It was there that my mother bought me my first guitar. We were staying in a small pensiõn near Chiavari and she had noticed my interest in the evening entertainment antics of two waiters who played acoustic guitars and sang songs to the guests. Those were the days before disco and karaoke. The waiters tolerated my incessant questions about their instruments and even let me sit with one on my knee to strum the open strings while they sang one of their songs. I don't suppose the crowd were particularly impressed but I was smitten. I knew little about the craft of playing music at the time and guitar chord structures were as yet completely unknown. I did have a sense, however, that one day I would buy a guitar for myself. Then my mother took me completely by surprise. She nipped into Chiavari one afternoon and returned with a guitar. For *me*! And although I had no idea how to play the damned thing, I returned from the holiday with pride and a determination to *get stuck in*. And did I? Oh, yes indeed.

I believe I was destined to play the guitar from the age of about five or six. In or around 1959, entertainers like Tommy Steele and Lonnie Donegan appeared on television shows which I vividly remember. Whenever Tommy or Lonnie came on I would pick up a plastic, child sized, tennis racquet and pretend it was a guitar and I'd 'play along' whenever they performed on the shows. Later, in 1964 as a 2nd Mirfield boy scout, I played air guitar (was I the unwitting forerunner of the craze?) at a Christmas party to which a local company of Guides and Brownies had been invited. I was Ray Davies of The Kinks on that occasion, air-guitaring along on stage to "You Really Got Me". It gets worse, though! Readers may remember The Val Doonican Show on tv. Val's knitted jumpers and rocking chair were his classic trademarks. But it was his lovely Gretsch guitar on which he strummed 'Little Boxes', "Rafferty's Motor Car', Delaney's Donkey' et al that I craved. So yes, unconsciously, I suppose I had always harboured a desire to play throughout my formative life. Thanks mam.

I had visited Northern Ireland only once during the 'troubles' but it was at a time when it was considered reasonably safe to do so. Vigilance was paramount, however, and at a checkpoint leading from the riverside area that would later become the magnificent Waterfront Hall and The Peace Bridge which crosses the river Lagan, I found myself compelled to gaze upon the still-life form of a sentried British soldier. I had caught his eye from the checkpoint queue and he caught mine. I was taken by how very young he looked; eighteen? nineteen? twenty? It was difficult to tell under the dull green helmet, shatterproof visor and dispassionate grey eyes devoid of any semblance of emotion. What images and memories might lie concealed behind those steely pupils were too dreadful to contemplate. There I was, confronted by this young man, a fellow countryman, nervous, alert and scrutinising everyone with suspicion. This soldier before me, no more than a boy, armed and unquestionably capable of immediate defensive reaction if the need arose, had no hint of my peaceful intentions or whether I might be his next violent encounter. The government had commanded his presence there long before I had become aware of organisations such as the IRA, UDA, RUC, INLA et al. I have no doubt though that he, by necessary contrast, was very much aware. Our passive encounter brought to mind the words from a verse in a song I'd once heard the actor and comedian Billy Connolly sing. The song tells of a British soldier injured and lying in hospital reflecting on his tour of Northern Ireland...

"I've a brother in England with long curly hair,
When I joined up he said I was daft.
He said shootin' strangers just wasn't his game
That brother o' mine is nae soft.
Well I can put up with most things I've done in my time.
I can even put up with the pain.
But what do you do with a gun in your hand
When you're facing a hundred odd weans?"

In my mid twenties a series of industrial disputes between the government and nurses, fire fighters and the miners made me begin considering issues beyond the bias of large sections of the printed press. My considerations, though, remained both basic and naive. Along with the majority of people I had no notion that I was being hoodwinked by a manipulative and powerful print media. But yet, a fixation was developing within. I had a growing sense that something wasn't right. Dramatic newspaper headlines alongside strategically cropped photographs went unchallenged in the main and my life drifted along with no attempt at any

11

detailed analysis of news stories. A majority of people, as always and even now, unquestioningly accept the opinions of a number of jingoistic newspaper owners who, along with many of their writers, all too often side with the whims and fancies of right wing governments as part of an Establishment policy of stirring populous prejudice.

Of course I had no concept of any of this at the time. Those who I considered more knowledgeable than myself opined about this, that and the other but I rarely engaged in their discussions for fear of exposing my youthful naivety. Instead I silently self questioned what I was hearing and held my own counsel. I know now, of course, that a lot of what I was hearing was merely opinionated, bigoted posturing. It's still the same today.

My turning point was reached in 1984. Paula Jo Barker, a friend from Oklahoma visiting the UK and later to settle here with dual citizenship, told me that, *"back home, people cannot understand why you British stand by while your government wages war on its own people".* She was referring to the then industrial dispute between the National Union of Mineworkers led by its President, Arthur Scargill, and the conservative government led by Prime Minister, Margaret Thatcher. Paula Jo's words resonated. Around the same time a workplace colleague unwittingly yet abruptly brought about further profound changes to my perception of life in Britain. I was on a break from work and resting in the television lounge adjacent to the restaurant in Darlington's Royal Mail Centre. The long running and increasingly bitter dispute between the miners and the government had reached its nadir and the television was showing scenes from the dispute on the lunchtime news. A handful of fellow postmen and postwomen were watching too, killing what free time they had left before returning to work. The images were of the terrible, violent clashes at Orgreave colliery near Sheffield where hundreds of striking miners were pitched against lines of baton wielding policemen, numbered in hundreds too, and with many on horseback. The level of violence meted out by both sides was awful to see. From where I was sitting at the back of the lounge I commented loudly, *"Bloody anarchy! It's bloody anarchy!"* That brief outburst led to a response which was to determine my future political thinking and direction. One of my supervisors, the socialist minded Bill Robinson, Darlington Borough councillor and Labour Party member, rose abruptly from his seat and declared in the angriest of voices, *"That's not bloody anarchy! It's people fighting for their jobs!"*

The impact was immediate. Switching my gaze alternately between Bill and the tv it slowly dawned on me what he meant. Everything which had been impossible for me to articulate became crystal clear at that point – 'war on people! fighting for jobs!'

I knew where I wanted my life to go from then on...

1 – Class Of '68

Class 4A at Woodhouse Close Secondary Modern School in Bishop Auckland queued disorderly and noisily while waiting to go in to the weekly music lesson. Our teacher, Mr.Elton, was late. Mr.Elton, or "Spike" as we referred to him because of his close cropped crew cut hair, was often late thus unwittingly encouraging our immature and impatient high volume chatter to pervade the long corridor. Teenage students should never be left waiting and expected to remain silent and orderly. 4A were a prime example. With one or two exceptions, girls mainly, our thirty strong 1968 class of fifteen and sixteen year olds were particularly vocal at the best of times.

Mr.Sutherland, tall, dark rim spectacled teacher of geography, stepped out from his classroom a few doors away. His face was as sharp as the creases in his beige cavalry twill slacks and as grave as his neatly woven dark brown checked jacket.

"What on earth is all this noise about?" he shouted above the din.

"Nothing, sir", replied two or three mumbling voices at the immediate cessation of noise.

One boy offered, "Mr.Elton's late, sir. And the room's locked."

"Well, keep the noise down. I'm trying to teach in here and I can hardly hear myself think!"

As soon as the geography room door closed our cacophony resumed. It was as if the click of the closing door had erased all memory of the minor telling off we had just received. But before further admonishment from "Baz" Sutherland, Mr.Elton came huffing, puffing and hurriedly scurrying along and without acknowledging our disorderly company, unlocked the door to our lesson.

I liked music lessons. Not for the soppy singing, though. All that '*By yon bonny banks and by yon bonny brae's*' stuff was sickly pathetic to my teenage mind and I mimed my way through most of those lessons. I liked Mr.Elton, though. When he had arrived a year earlier there was no more soppy singing. In one fell swoop music lessons became relevant and fun. He was the one who brought in Bob Dylan's LP "Freewheeling" and he took us through the meaning of songs such as Masters Of War...

"Come you Masters Of War,
You that build all the guns,
You that build the death planes,
You that build all the bombs,
You that hide behind walls,
You that hide behind desks,
I just want you to know I can see through your masks".

Contemporary, stirring stuff that made you think, question and open up your mind. As a teenager I thought, "Yeah. This is *it*! Give me *more*". I learned that simple E minor song and used it years later at gigs. There was one occasion where Spike contrasted Beethoven's Eroica Symphony with The Beatle's Sgt.Pepper album. We listened to both in entirety over two or three lessons. What a man. Crazy. I loved him.

"Right! In you go. Quietly now."

We shuffled in as instructed but chatting noisily, moving and rearranging chairs as we went.

"I said, quietly! Graham! Philip Graham! What have I just said?"

"Quietly, sir,"

The classroom fell silent.

"Yes. I did. So does that give you permission to carry on talking?"

"No, sir."

"So, why did you?"

"Why did I what, sir."

"Don't be funny with me, lad. Why did you carry on talking?"

"It wasn't just me, sir." I protested.

"No. It never is just you". His voice was angrier now. "It's always someone else, isn't it?"

"No, sir".

"What do you mean, lad?" His face reddened as the inquisition grew louder. "You just said, 'no, sir'.

"I didn't sir. I mean, I did..."

"Sit down. And don't let me hear another peep from you this day."

Our particularly cross music teacher turned and made his way to the piano and instructed us to open our books to a song or other such page relevant to where we were in that autumn term. I watched him sorting sheets of music before neatly placing them on the piano shelf.

"Sir", I said raising my hand.

"Yes, Graham? I thought I said I didn't want to hear from you anymore!"

"I know, sir. But does that mean I shouldn't sing today as well?"

That did it. My impudence tipped him over the edge. Slamming down the lid of the piano and startling those not paying attention, Spike Elton, more red faced now, rose swiftly to his feet and screamed fearsomely.

"Out! Get out! Go on, lad. Get out! And wait for me in the hall."

I needed no persuading. Whatever had brought on Spike's stress that morning had been made a lot worse by my presence. I made my way to the school assembly hall dreading what might yet befall me.

To this day I hold fast to the belief that challenging unfairness, injustice and wrongdoing, wherever it may be encountered, is the right thing to do; although now, as an older person, I restrain myself somewhat having a thought for being beaten up or slashed with a knife. But in school, if a teacher said or did anything which I felt was incorrect or unjust, I would be the one to ask them to justify their claim or action. Later, as an adult, I would bring up my own two sons to adopt a similar maxim. Such mannerisms didn't make me popular of course and with the exception of my wonderful, understanding and perceptive English teacher, Mrs.Hardisty, who understood me better than most, I was the constantly questioning gadfly in the ears of others.

'Betty' Hardisty, had long tolerated my outspokenness but unlike her counterparts she worked to harness my exuberance for challenge and question, seeing the trait as potentially positive if honed and directed. As well as dealing with the whole class, in personal conversations she would encourage me to adhere to the use of 'good' English while engaging me in all manner of out of school topics. That's the reason, by way of just one example, why I get pedantic over the incorrect use of the word 'of' when 'have' is correct. People, who today roll their eyes when I pick up on grammatical error, have Betty Hardisty to blame... not I.

I could take liberties with Betty and often did. Once when the class had been particularly bothersome and not all were paying attention, Betty snapped. She was livid and ordered one boy, David Woodgate, out of the classroom before commanding the rest of us to report for detention at the end of the school day. Bugger! I had a drama class that evening and was concerned that detention would make me late. I considered simply not turning up for the detention but I knew my absence would be noticed. A more cunning plan was required. During the afternoon break and knowing that the English room was not needed for the final session of the day, I crept in and wrote on the board, "No detention today 4A" and signed it, EH. I would have loved to have been a fly on the wall when EH discovered an empty classroom and the chalk written message. I was never found out although I think she knew.

There was another occasion in school where I felt I was being unjustly hauled over the coals. It occurred during a history lesson given by Mr."Nobby" Clark. My alleged misdemeanour? Dirty fingerprints on the class register that I had been asked to go and fetch after Nobby had forgotten to bring it himself. Now, those dirty fingerprints weren't mine but I knew whose they were. Nonetheless, I was not one for snitching. I explained to him that the prints were on the register when I had collected it from the staff room. At least I *tried* to explain.

"What's this?" Nobby demanded sharply to no one in particular. He held aloft the dirtied front cover to the assembled class and stood before us with glazed eyes and his body noticeably trembling.

"I don't know how some people live these days. I really don't! I taught some of your parents, you know? That's right, I did. Yours, Robinson. And yours, too. Are you listening, Askwith?"

"Yes sir!"

"Well, look as if you are, then."

There followed the briefest pause in his outrage.

"I often wonder how people turn out. Look at this for example", he beckoned frantically waving the register before his silenced cohort.

"But they're not my fingerprints, sir."

"Be quiet", he snapped staring me full in the face. And then, pausing once more, he took a deep breath, rose up on his toes and then slowly settled back down. You could have heard a pin drop as we waited for his next outburst.

"Some of you. You, in particular, Graham, will leave here one day and wish you'd listened a lot more. That's right. You will. But it'll be too late by then. Too late. None of you have any idea what life is like. And most of you would probably shit yourselves if we still had conscription."

Conscription? Where the hell did that come from? And he said 'shit' as well. Two or three barely stymied sniggers was all it took for the rest of us to start giggling. In a matter of seconds Nobby's increasingly frantic and angry shouts were drowned out by an orchestra of uncontrolled, side splitting laughter. It was impossible to stop. Once the 'shit' word had been uttered we were completely beyond control and poor Nobby lost all wit and whim to bring us back to order. We were still in fits and stitches when our deadly earnest history teacher sat down at his desk, rolled back his head and gave out a ruttled snore. That set us off again. But not for long. Nobby Clark was having a heart attack.

Mr.Elton entered the vast assembly hall and walked noisily across the polished wooden floor. I heard his rhythmic footsteps approaching down the centre aisle of uniformly placed seats which separated the boys from the girls. He approached where I was seated, head down in pitiful, reflective silence in front of the massive, purple curtained stage. He sat down next to me and I felt his presence while not daring to look up. Time slowed as the icy quiet between us began to thaw. He spoke first. Quietly and calmly.

"Right, Philip. Look at me. Look at me while I'm talking."

I raised my head and stared into his florid face. I was taken aback to see the evident kindness in his adult blue eyes and my boyish fears subsided a little.

"What is it with you, Philip?" he asked gently.

"What do you mean, sir?"

"I'll tell you what I mean, Philip. You're a bright lad with good prospects..."

"Thank you, sir."

"Don't interrupt", he cut in. We were now eye to eye. "I see in you a free spirit, a lone wolf, an eagle flying high..."

I had no idea what he meant and I felt uncomfortable again and thinking that he was off his trolley.

"It seems to me, though", he continued, "that you challenge things just a little too much. A lot of the staff say that about you, you know? You are a good lad in general but you always have something to say. It's got to stop, Philip. If it doesn't, well I'm afraid one day it will get you into a lot of trouble."

"But sir, that's not fair. I only ask about things I don't understand and if I'm being picked on and it's not my fault I'll say so."

"I know, Philip. I know."

More moments of perplexing silence followed.

"Can I come back into music, sir? Please!"

"Alright", he sighed rising from his seat and staring down at me. "But, please, Philip. No more backchat, eh?"

"But sir", I persisted as he stiffened. "Imagine if you were me this morning. How would you feel if you were being picked on as the only one talking when there were others just as bad?"

He paused before replying.

"You know, Philip. You should go into politics"....

2 – A Change Of Direction

My first job after leaving school in May 1969 was at the button factory, Ernest & Henry Ltd, on St.Helen's Trading Estate. I owe that to my stepgrandfather Charles Mitchinson, a retired coal miner who had married my widowed gran in 1961. He took me around the factories asking to speak to managers where, enamoured by his pro-activeness I suppose, some people actually invited us in and I explained that I was waiting for my GCSE exam results and looking for work. Grandad's strategy paid off and, at Ernest & Henry Ltd, I was offered a job doing general office duties. It was also the day that I had my first cigarette.

"Here you go, son", he said as we stepped off the bus on our way home. "You're almost sixteen now so here's a packet of fags for you."

I didn't become a heavy smoker and thankfully I gave up altogether more than thirty years ago. Everybody seemed to smoke in those days and it would have been highly likely that I would have started anyway without the kickstart from grandad. But what a feeling! I felt so grown up. Looking back I can't thank him for buying me those cigarettes, the smoke and smell of which I now despise, but what he did in getting me in front of some of the local employers was priceless.

As soon as I got my exam results – English Language (A), English Literature (A), Art (A), Geography (B), Technical Drawing (B), Maths, Science and History (all D's) - I went to the Careers Office in Craddock Street, today a private residence, in the Cockton Hill area of town. I sat with my mother while an unsmiling, horn rim spectacled middle aged woman flicked through a file of cards indicating where job vacancies existed and where my recently acquired academic effort might be put to use. I eyed the manner in which she was dressed; dark brown skirted suit devoid of fashion or sex appeal and so thickly woven it could surely have kept an Icelandic fisherman warm. After a staccato of verbal exchanges wherein my input was largely ignored, we eventually settled on a card seeking local government officers in Durham. Both my mother and the careers advisor felt the job would be eminently suitable for me and I was given an application form and a pre-paid envelope. Even with my mother asking most of the questions, we were given a paucity of further information before being sent on our way.

So then, in September 1969, having left the button factory, I was suited, booted and desk bound in the Secondary Education Department at County Hall in Durham. I was given an insight into school transport, school meals, sports and recreation while ferrying papers back and forth to the typing pool, the shop and the stationery stores. I found

26

nothing particularly engaging and boredom quickly set in. A couple of years later I transferred to the Area Education Office in Spennymoor under the managership of the straight laced, military style composure of one Albert Trennery. Different workplace, same boredom. Although, to be fair, being amongst just five or six others as opposed to hundreds in Durham, the atmosphere was lighter and more comradely. Nevertheless, I left in 1972 before I would almost certainly have been dismissed for general immaturity and lack of application to my job. I then found employment in Bishop Auckland as a Purchase Ledger clerk with Westool Engineering Ltd. The move was nothing more than 'out of the frying pan and into the fire' and I was dismissed in due course for absenteeism. I went from Westool to the accounts department at R & W A Johnson Builders in Willington from where I was again dismissed for not returning after a period of leave and finally, after a brief spell on the dole, to Wheeler's Heating & Fabrications in Newton Aycliffe. Not exactly a great start to a life of work, eh?

Truth be known, as a teenager I lacked any significant direction in life. My father had been killed in a car crash when I was twelve and my mother worked long hours to provide for herself and my brother and me. I went out a lot. Home was where I slept and left for school or work. For four or five years, whilst not engaging in criminal or antisocial activities, I was nevertheless feral to some extent spending just about every evening and weekend with my then girlfriend, Barbara Laycock. Barbara lived with her family on Eldon Bank near Shildon. During this time I had very little contact with my brother, Andy, who had his own circle of friends plus, to be honest, a lot of the time that I spent with my mother saw us arguing. I had no mentor, no guidance and I pretty much got on with whatever I wanted to do. Because of this I was looked upon by some as immature, vain and selfish. How's that for a confession?

In September 1974, at just twenty one years old, I had been signing on the dole for three months. My services had been deemed no longer required at Wheeler's Fabrications in Aycliffe where I had worked in the accounts department. It was the briefest of employments, having only been there for nine weeks, and I recall the head of personnel requesting my presence and telling me that the economy and the business' revenues weren't good and that savings needed to be made.

"If and when things pick up, Phil, I'd like to think we can call you back."

I didn't detect any sense of sincerity in what he said and Wheeler's went out of business shortly after. And no... it had nothing to do with my inexperience with their accounts. At least, I don't think so!!

Like a million or so others at that time I was now having a hard time finding a job and it didn't take long for the fortnightly ritual of signing on the dole to become indelibly ingrained in that pitiless, concrete and glass, eight storey edifice known as Vinovium House.

At the time I lived in Bishop Auckland high up on the town's council built Woodhouse Close Estate. My family, comprising my widowed mother, myself and Andy, were the first occupants in January 1966 of no.16 Weardale Drive, one of several houses in a red brick terrace with front and rear gardens. From there a regular United town service bus, the number nine as we knew it and rival company, OK Motor Services, took just ten minutes or so to-ing and fro-ing between the estate and the town centre from where, a few years later, I took the short walk to the dole office.

In many ways I was more fortunate than some who queued to sign on as I had been placed on what was known as the PER, the Professional Executive Register. I was on the register due to my employment in the accounts departments of my previous two jobs. The rationale behind the PER was that whilst signing on and encouraged to take up the offer of employment in any industry, shop or workplace which came along, a small team of clerks were assigned to assist my return to the clerical world of purchase ledger, sales ledger, profit & loss and payroll. I didn't quite feel like an executive, but the soubriquet was mildly pleasing.

On my way to sign on one dull September morning, I bumped into Gordon Hopwood, a friend from school. Gordon and I had maintained contact as we entered the world of work, he as a postman, following in his father's footsteps, and myself in local government and accounts. Gordon was often present at gigs which Victoria, the rock and pop group I had recently joined as bass guitarist played and so our post-school relationship was maintained. Knowing I was out of work Gordon told me that the GPO, as it was known before changing years later to Royal Mail, was advertising for casual labour to work over the busy Christmas period. In those days, more so than now in our fully automated postal industry, 'casuals' were intrinsic to the manual sorting, handling and delivering of the much higher mail volumes over the Christmas period. I wasn't overly keen but Gordon persuaded me that I'd be okay and that it would provide a source of income where there was none at present save for my dole money. What little money I earned from playing in Victoria went on cigarettes, late night chinese suppers and bottles of looney soup in the guise of Newcastle Brown Ale. I wasn't one for saving money but my social life, although limited to the band, was reasonably okay. After signing on I called in to the Post Office counter on the town's Tenter Street and came away with an application form.

The letter inviting me to an interview came within a few days. I was to report to the GPO, again on Tenter Street and to the rear of the Post Office counter, at 10:30am the following Tuesday and to be prepared for a maths and mental agility test. The interview would last approximately one hour and twenty minutes and I couldn't help think that this was a lot of palaver for two or three weeks casual employment.

As interviews go it wasn't bad. I detected straight away a military feel to the proceedings. This shouldn't have been at all surprising as in those days many former military personnel found their way into the GPO where people had 'ranks' and performed 'duties' and where every document, form and item of equipment had a number and an acronym. Even something as basic as a GPO pen was an SP15. Sounds like sunscreen, doesn't it?

I was introduced to the PE'C', Alan Wall, by his PE'D', Dickie Wilkinson. Alan, a tall and stockily framed man with short, neatly combed hair was in his fifties I summised. He wore a smart dark blue blazer and neatly pressed grey trousers and came across as friendly and welcoming. Dickie, also friendly and welcoming, slightly older than Alan, was in the serge blue uniform of the time with two brass crowns, one on each lapel to signify his elevated status in the organisation.

Hierarchy in the GPO began with postmen and postwomen (PMN and PWN) progressing, if ambitious, to the now disbanded Postman/woman Higher Grade (PHG) where most of one's duties were based indoors. Next came Supervisory PHG (S/PHG) where an element of supervision formed part of the job and then Postal Executive Grade D (PE'D) being wholly supervisory until attaining the dizzy heights to assume sole charge of an office as PE'C. There were grades above PE'C but for all intents and purposes these were the five main grades in the vast majority of delivery offices at that time. All these grades were changed in the last two decades of the twentieth century when Royal Mail began operating as a business destroying at a stroke a highly regarded and respected public service. It was then that PMN and PWN became OPG's which is Operational Postal Grade, PHG's were scrapped altogether and PE'D's became managers, wearing suits and ties instead of the once ubiquitous grey cotton dustcoats. Delivery office PE'D's were given the title of DOM, for Delivery Office Manager, and their DOM counterparts in the new Mail Centres assumed the ranks of Processing Mangers and Distribution managers with the designations JV which referred to the rather mundane 'Job Value'. There are many former PMN and PWN alive today who would attest to the fact that, with some notable exceptions, the bestowed title of manager was greater than many an ability in respect of how some JV's managed their people.

But that was the way the 'business' was destined to go and when it did many a friendly and supportive former supervisor became a watcher for slackers, more inclined towards a sense of overblown importance as opposed to one of the lads and lasses on the front line. Indeed, the parlous state of industrial relations in the UK postal industry in the last thirty or so years that I worked there, once relatively benign, can be traced back to the time when supervisors became managers and the postal service became a business. Disputes of a personal and workplace nature grew at such a rate across the country that it got to a point in 1993 where a government commission was set up under the authority of Lord Tom Sawyer to look into the state of industrial relations within the postal industry. Sawyer's commission took a year to complete and his finished report did not make comfortable reading for either management or union. His findings, however, led to the establishment in September 1994 of a nationally agreed Industrial Relations Framework, a document designed through the clarity and simplicity of its text to avoid confrontation and, where such failed, provided a step by step process to resolve whatever issue was to hand. Alas, as helpful as the IR Framework is, and in spite of the nationally agreed and binding authority it contains, it quickly became disliked and generally ignored by many managers and used as a weapon by the union.

The IR Framework, however, was years away from inception when, on the day of my interview, I promptly felt at ease and sailed through the initial question and answer session and the maths. The mental agility test was amusing, though, with pictures being shown to me of such things as a

33

bicycle with the chain attached to the front wheel as opposed to the rear. The objective was to spot such idiosyncrasies. I left with handshakes and a promise that I would hear from them in the next few days. However, during the interview a significant point was raised by both Alan and Dickie. They wanted to know about my outside interests and immediately took an interest in my playing in a rock and roll band... or 'group' as they were known then.

"It's just that we start early, you know", said Alan. "We've just had to get rid of a lad who plays in a group because he was always sleeping in."

I knew full well who they were referring to. It was Victoria's drummer, my future brother in law, Alan Rowley. Alan had earlier confided in me that he had "had to leave" the GPO as the early mornings were becoming a problem. I kept my thoughts to myself in the presence of my interviewers acknowledging only that I knew Alan Rowley from school. I lied that he wasn't in my group, and that the group I was currently in didn't have any gigs over the Christmas period. I lied about that, too.

The letter informing me that I had been successful arrived in the first post on Friday morning offering me a job as a postman subject to a satisfactory medical and the signing of Section 2 of the Official Secrets Act. It then went on to indicate a start date of Wednesday 16th October and that I would be working forty three hours a week on a full time contract. At that point I didn't know whether to laugh or cry, celebrate or commiserate. What I had failed to notice on the 'casual' application form I had filled out a couple of weeks earlier was that it was for a *full time* postal job and that that's what I would now be doing... for the next thirty four years.

My first three days, in the company of other new recruits, was spent initially in a day long induction class learning about the service, rules and regulations, procedures, discipline, annual leave, sick and special leave plus a presentation by the Union of Post Office Workers representative, Charlie Elliot. There then followed two days of 'dead' sorting. Dead sorting is the practice of standing in front of a forty eight box wooden frame into which addressed 'training cards' are sorted. We were given a brief introduction to the destination designated to each box and allowed an hour or so to sort the cards and become familiarised with the destinations. There are two types of sorting – inward and outward. Inward sorting is the practise of sorting mail to local boxes addressed within the area covered by the Delivery Office. In regard to Bishop Auckland this included Cockton Hill East, Cockton Hill West, Town Centre, Tindale Crescent, Eldon Lane, Auckland Park, South Church, Coundon and many more. Outward sorting, by contrast, was for the regions, cities and towns and around the country - Edinburgh, Bristol, Leeds, Manchester, Wales and the Marches etc, along with an Air

Mail box. After familiarisation we were timed for sorting speeds of which there was a required standard of, if I remember correctly, about eighteen items per minute. Once our cards had been sorted the contents of random boxes were checked for accuracy by a PHG. Having passed the sorting tests we were measured for our uniforms and then sent home for the weekend to anxiously wait for Monday morning when we'd be let loose, supervised of course, on our first mail delivery. Now my new job would begin in earnest.

I joined the Union of Post Office Workers straight away, although to be honest, in those early days, I really didn't know or care much about the benefits of membership. Industrial disputes in the UK have long been unjustly but inexorably attributed to trade unions, more often than not a convenient misconception pedalled by sections of the media, conservative ministers, their MP's and more than a few ignorant and unscrupulous employers and business leaders. In actual fact, as I soon learned, aside from representation in disciplinary matters, the social benefits of joining a trade union are many and worthwhile with low interest loans, advice and help with faulty purchases, free legal and medical services, discounts on holidays, goods and shopping to name but some. But perhaps the most welcome social benefit in the postal trade union is the one which its members never get to see... a death benefit paid to a nominated next of kin to help towards funeral costs. Macabre? Not at all. The death benefit is a worthy and welcome payment to families at such an unsettling time. I would come to value the wide cover and protection that the union provided. But for now I simply turned up for duty, became more and more familiar with the delivery areas, or walks as they are known, and knuckled down to doing my job.

Most days I'd start at five in the morning having risen at quarter past four. This was no easy accomplishment at first but with the aid of a newly purchased alarm clock I managed to get up and out each morning with a little time to spare once I arrived at the delivery office. Being late was frowned upon although unofficially permissible for a period up to five minutes. Supervising PHG's were partly responsible with the PE'D for making sure everyone had turned up for work and on time, their SP15 pens poised in readiness to scribble two damning red crosses next to late attendee duty numbers on the signing-in sheet. Too many late attendances of more than five minutes triggered an action as proscribed in the relevant section of the Head Postmasters Manual, a voluminous 'bible' containing every aspect of the job in minute detail and applicable to all ranks and grades. Warning interviews invariably followed the 'lates' with a range of disciplinary measures meted out for further or persistent transgressions. Of course, the chief problem with being late for duty was the knock on effect to the delayed delivery of the mail. The timing of walks in those days was determined in law by the Post Office Act where none could commence before 7am and with the objective of ensuring as much mail as possible was delivered before people had left for work. Who remembers those halcyon days? It remains a source of intense irritation to me that the onset of politically driven, dogmatic privatisation has sold, on the cheap, a once highly respected public service to individuals and institutions whose sole interest is in capital gain and sod the service to the public. And has the service got better? Not at all. Deliveries are now much later in the day and the service is more expensive to use. And, as it seems to me, this applies to every other privatised industry that once offered reliable and affordable public services. And the fact that Joe and Josephine public was invited to join in these UK sell-offs makes it even more galling. But there we have it. Just don't twist on to me about how bad things are with Gas, Electricity, Water, Railways, sections of the National Health Service to name but a few. Thousands of people *took the privatisation shilling* which, instead of leading to sound investment, led to higher prices and poorer service. Live with it.

For sleeping in, those who had a telephone at home were rung from their beds whereas those without telephones suffered the ignominy and embarrassment of a GPO van arriving at their home to be loudly door-knocked - an action which often woke next door neighbours, too.

My first three days on delivery, starting at the east of the town at Coronation and taking in Bridge Place, Eldon Lane, Coundon Grange, Close House and Eldon Bank, was undertaken with an experienced and most helpful postman, Tommy Pinder. The delivery, thanks to Tommy's patient tuition and advice, was relatively straightforward with only a couple of misdeliveries when out on my own over Thursday to Saturday. A major problem facing those who deliver the mail is that of dogs. Believe me, even the most placid doe-eyed pooch can be a vicious and determined protector of property when a postie comes along.

"It's alright," dog owners often laugh. "He won't bite!" before, "No, Bruiser! No! Bad dog. Let go! No! No! Get in the fucking house you bad dog." And then, "Eeeh, I'm ever so sorry. He never usually goes for anyone. Here, let me wipe the blood..."

Placing fingers through letterboxes is a sure fire way of being bitten. A friend of mine, Walter Mackley, had his fingers so badly bitten that he had to undergo surgery. Returning to work several weeks later, he was attacked by two dogs while walking down a street in Leeholme. Such were his injuries to his upper legs and arms, although mainly superficial this time, he was never again the confident postman of old. And then, where some might say he hadn't learned his lesson, Walter was bitten again putting mail

39

through a letterbox sustaining further bites to his previously injured fingers. Did that ever happen to Postman Pat?

The GPO had a system in place for dealing with dangerous dogs. If a postman or postwoman perceived there to be a threat from a dog in a garden or on business premises, they could refuse to enter and return the mail to the delivery office endorsed and signed with the words, "Dog Loose". The S/PHG or PE'D would then write an officially worded letter to the addressee advising that mail could not be guaranteed for delivery unless the dog was secured and under control. Guess who then had to attempt to deliver the letter? That's right. If it wasn't so serious I'd make a joke out if it.

Dog attacks, often the butt of jokes and the subject of newspaper and magazine cartoons, are serious matters with many weeks each year lost to recovery from bites. Some people never fully recover from the injuries they sustain. As a consequence the union, under the leadership of National Health & Safety Officer, Dave Joyce, was instrumental in lobbying Parliament and meeting ministers to bring into law the current Dangerous Dogs Act. That it took nearly fifteen years into the new millennium to achieve, and whilst indicative of the pioneering approach to health and safety by a trade union, it is a damning indictment of the slow progress towards postal workers' welfare and safety by successive governments of either colour.

Misdeliveries, by the way, are where mail is put through the wrong letterbox. It often leads to charges of wilful delay, a crime leading to imprisonment for the most serious acts. This is where I had my first experience of union representation. Not long after being in the job I was summoned to interview about some misdeliveries and at which I was permitted to be accompanied by my union representative, Charlie Elliot. Charlie spoke on my behalf because of my being relatively new to the job, calling for common sense to prevail in that I was indeed new, not just to the job but to the geography of many of the walks. A tense twenty four hours passed as I waited for the decision of my PE'D inquisitor. In the end I was let off with no warning entry on my records. The experience, however, gave me my first indication that discipline procedures were deadly serious affairs, played by the book and not to be caught up in if one could help it. Would I have been let off so leniently without the input of the union? Perhaps. Perhaps not.

Ribald tales of bored, alluring housewives have entered the British psyche thanks to a number of films, tv, radio, plays and books. It's a genre of comedy that I find unfunny and grossly overdone for nothing more than male titillation. Except...one morning I had to knock at a door to obtain a signature for a registered delivery item. While waiting patiently I saw a curtain move and out of the corner of my eye I caught a fleeting glimpse of a naked woman. Had I

41

imagined it? Not at all. The front door opened and there, right before my eyes, stood an attractive woman in her late thirties or early forties wearing nothing but the briefest of pink panties.

"Yes!", she enquired without embarrassment or attempt to conceal her nudity.

"Erm", I stuttered. "I have a registered item for you to sign for."

The lady sighed, rolled her eyes and reached for the signing slip and my pen.

"This always happens when my husband's away. Every bloody time. Come in while I find something to rest on."

"Er. No. I think I'd better stay here, thank you." I struggled to avoid staring at her well developed breasts while noticeably aroused as any twenty one year old fella might be. I was nervous as hell.

"Oh, well. Wait there, then. I shalln't be long."

I watched her as she sashayed down the hallway to the kitchen, rested the slip on a table, signed it and then slowly and alluringly returned to me. I took the slip and handed her the item.

"Are you sure you…"

"Thanks. I need to get going", I spluttered in the most ridiculously adolescent manner. "Have a good day."

And, with that, I left hurriedly as she closed the door on our brief erotic encounter.

The chummy mayhem of Christmas deliveries came and went and the introduction to the new year saw me making good progress. By the end of March there was talk of placing me on driving duties, an exciting prospect which would lead to more pay through the allocation of a weekly driving allowance. There was an obstacle to this exciting prospect, however, in that I couldn't drive. It was to my surprise then that I learned there was a national agreement between the UPW and the GPO which provided release from duty without loss of pay to undertake in-house driving tuition, free of charge, eight hours a day for five consecutive days with the driving test being sat the following Monday. I promptly applied for my provisional license.

Such intense daily tuition, no week-long break in between lessons as on civvy street, meant the pass rate was high. I failed. I failed reversing around corners using wing mirrors. In spite of several faltering attempts I either ventured too far over to the middle of the road or mounted the nearside kerb. It should have mattered. Indeed it might have if a new date wasn't immediately set for me to go through the whole process again, eight hours a day over five days and a test the following Monday. This time I passed. Imagine what the cost would be today! Eighty hours of driving tuition and two tests! Postmen and Postwomen in the modern Royal Mail business have none of the driving support I was given all those years ago.

While waiting for the rescheduled lessons I had been encouraged to accompany the afternoon and evening collection drivers as they drove around the towns and countryside collecting mail from sub post offices emptying post boxes enroute. With L plates duly affixed I drove many a collection route with the duty holder sat alongside as my mentor. One notable postman I drove for was Alan Parker. Short and stocky in stature, Alan could have been a successful stand up comedian such was the extent of his joke and gag vocabulary. He had my sides aching along many country lanes. At the same time, however, he was experienced enough to know that I needed to learn a few things about the collections and, in particular, about driving. It was Alan who patiently showed me how to correctly reverse around corners using wing mirrors. I thank him to this day as being the one, more than any instructor, who got me through my second test.

And yet there's an astonishing coda. Having passed the test I was permitted, again as part of an agreement between the union and employer, to take a spare van and drive anywhere I liked for up to two hours a day not exceeding ten hours over the week... and then claim it as overtime!

3 – See You In Court

When I became a postman I was also playing bass guitar in a quite successful rock and pop band called Victoria. We were good and had a large and loyal following around the clubs and pubs of Tyneside and Wearside with occasional forays into south Yorkshire and across to Cumbria. Being 'on the road', living a weekend rock and roll lifestyle, was tremendous fun and I never thought for one moment that it would ever end. The four of us, Robert Gittins, brothers Alan and Graham Rowley and myself all had regular jobs, although Alan had recently been sacked from the GPO, remember? and Graham was still at school. We gave up our weekends to performing. Our hedonistic excesses were exacting but with youth on our side we had scant care while dashing recklessly through life caught up in the wildest of teenage dreams. Our manager, Basil Smith, Shildon based husband of freelance journalist, Dorothy Smith, often despaired at our antics before and after a show. He never chastised us, however. Basil accepted that we were young and oblivious to any useful sense of responsibility. As long as we remained on the right side of criminality he was happy to let us indulge ourselves just so long as our stage performances didn't suffer. There was one time, however, when Basil called the four of us to a meeting. It was plain to see from the outset that he was not happy and we sensed something foreboding was about to be unleashed.

"When you played at that nurses party in the hospital last weekend", he began. "Did you use one of their staff rooms to get changed in?"

"Why aye", we chirped up together.

"Why? What's up?" asked Robert.

"Can you tell me what happened to the boxes of chocolates and bottles of alcohol?"

I think it was Robert again who answered.

"Why, yes. They were very generous in providing us with it all. We ate some chocolates, drank a bottle or two and brought the rest back home in the van."

Silence. And then...

"They weren't meant for you", said Basil in despair. "They were gifts to the nurses from relatives of terminally ill patients, you bloody idiots. Apart from the chocolates, which is bad enough, you've stolen two bottles of whiskey, two bottles of vodka, some vermouth and a brandy. And now the police are involved and treating it as theft!"

Quite how Basil resolved that little episode I have no idea. But he did. And we weren't questioned by the police or prosecuted. I hope my mother enjoyed her chocolates.

In time I came to realise that travelling and performing, often not arriving home till the early hours, was not conducive to holding down a job which required me to start

46

work at five o'clock in the morning. I started to sleep in occasionally and was generally permanently tired. My teenage dream was beginning to fade and I quit the group. It was a decision which I came to regret and still do today. Touring and playing with Victoria was, after all, great fun. Fun, that is, except when travelling home after a show with an over imbibed drummer. We travelled to gigs in the back of a Ford Transit van, a group staple of the time, driven by our friend Mick Cooper. Alan, our drummer, was a great fella sober but unpredictable and often volatile in drink. Whilst I could never have been described as a goody-two-shoes, I never felt it good form to drink openly on stage. My discreet tipple was always a rum with blackcurrant hidden away behind an amp or a PA column. Robert drank very little and then only before and after a show and Graham wasn't legally old enough. Alan, though, bless his memory, could pick up a pint glass from the floor next to his drum stool, take a swig and put it back down again without ever missing a beat. Sheer brilliance.

There are two stories of note concerning Alan and booze – at least where Victoria was concerned. One night at a club in Blyth and unbeknown to the rest of us, Alan negotiated with the club secretary to pay a proportion of our fee in crates of Newcastle Brown Ale. Imagine our incredulity when this secret deal came to light as we loaded up the van to head home. Did it piss us off? Yeah. But the funny side was quickly brought to the fore when we bought fish and chips and carried the Brown Ale on to the nearby beach, lit a camp fire and had a bloody good laugh while getting drunk with our crew and some locals.

The second incident sums up both Alan's drumming prowess and his love of strong beer. Occasionally, members of our families would travel with us to gigs. Alan's wife, my soon to be sister in law Janet, was with us one night in Newcastle and at one point, late in the show, Alan beckoned her to the front of the stage. As we played I saw Alan raise the palm of his hand towards Janet and I swear he was saying "only five minutes to go". Bloody fool that I am, of course. What he was actually saying was, "get me five pints and bring 'em here!" And, do you know what? She did precisely that. Returning back stage a short while later, she walked across to where Alan was playing and, carrying a tray which held five pints of Exhibition Ale, set them down by his drum stool. He drank the lot before the encore. I thought it sent out an unprofessional image. But what a star!

Away from Victoria, Alan and I were regular drinking buddies. I liked my share of the looney soup as much as he did and we would often be seen together around the pubs and workingmens' clubs of Shildon and Bishop Auckland. The trouble was, the drink often changed Alan from a happy chappy to depressed boor quick to fly into temper with me frequently on the receiving end of verbal outbursts and an occasional fist. But, all in all, they were great times. We were getting paid too, if not quite enough to make a living. That wasn't the point, though. For me the pleasure was then, and remains so today, of being on stage and seeing the audience responding and applauding our act. We were successful because we were considered a "bit earthy". I don't mean we swore on stage or anything like that but we never over-rehearsed. We got to know the songs and put our own stamp on them. This gave something of an edge to our music where people could relate to the songs as popular favourites of the time but with a slightly at odds feel to them. That's exactly what I do today with Share The Darkness and in, my view, it's a winning formula. A formula which has served me well for more than fifty years.

To be honest I grew to dislike a lot of the songs we played in Victoria. We became a 'club' act where the punters wanted to hear the same stuff they were used to hearing on the radio every day. I liked to rock it up a bit playing songs by Steppenwolfe, Nazareth, Status Quo and the like. Of course we had that stuff in our act, along with a couple of our own songs, but we always had to major on playing a lot of safe puerile shite like Tie A Yellow Ribbon Round The Old Oak Tree, Knock Three Times and, for goodness sake, Benny Hill's "Ernie, Who Drove The Fastest Milkcart In The West".

I mentioned Steppenwolfe, didn't I? We played a version of their hit "Born To Be Wild" at every gig, usually towards the latter part of the show. Alan and I had devised individual drum and bass solo's in the middle of the song which always went down well after the audience were sufficiently smashed on the drink. One day Basil suggested we ought to bring the song into the first set, solo's and all. We thought he was barking mad, of course. All that rock, drums and bass after Snoopy Versus The Red Baron and before Billy Don't Be A Hero was, to our mind, a recipe for disaster. How wrong we were. We gave it a go and it was just the thing to shake up the room after a quiet start and it gave audiences a taste of what was to come later after the bingo, raffle or whatever. Thank you, Basil.

Nevertheless, in spite of the soon to be realised regret, I felt I had made the right decision to quit when I did; not just for my job but because I was planning to buy a house and get married. Here, again, was another decision which I would come to regret.

I moved to Spennymoor Delivery Office in July 1975 having requested a transfer there after hearing they had a vacancy for a driver. In addition, with my future wife, Carole Campbell, sister of Alan Rowley's wife, Janet, we purchased No.11 Attwood Terrace in nearby Tudhoe Colliery. I left my family home on Woodhouse Close Estate, a departure which caused some minor tension between my mother and myself. Sadly, the tension remained down the years until the day she died in January 2012. Ah, well. That's family life I guess and not something I wish to go into here. Also at that time a Campbell family dispute over a Will meant Carole's widowed mother, Jean, had to vacate their family home in Spennymoor's Barnfield Road which she had lived in all her married life. I was now grappling with a mortgage, rates, electric and gas bills plus, before we had properly settled in, Jean came to live with us unwittingly setting the scene for three way domestic disharmony which would lead eventually to the breakdown of our marriage. Not that my then mother in law was the direct cause of the breakdown, but her input in our lives was always pervasive. Ironically, my brother in law Alan had warned me from the outset that it might happen. To make matters worse my sister in law, Janet, left Alan in 1980 and came with her three young children to live with us. We made them welcome, naturally, and did all we could to provide support and assistance throughout and beyond her eventual divorce. As I've said... family life!! Thankfully, my family life today is wonderful.

I walked confidently along Parkwood Precinct in Spennymoor to where I had been told to attend at 4.45am outside the public entrance to the Post Office Counter with its delivery office, my new workplace, to the rear. With only eighteen postmen, a Supervising PHG and a PE'D, I was looking forward to being part of this small band of new found colleagues. My initial anticipation was wiped away, however, with my first encounter with one Ossie Brown. Ossie, the Supervising PHG, sat casually on a bench, arms stretched out along the back and his legs and feet out in front so that his rather large stomach faced up to the sky. I was conscious of him eyeing me up as I made my way along and he offered neither a smile nor comment. No attempt whatsoever was given to acknowledge my arrival behind his cheerless grim faced stare. I offered a handshake which was taken half heartedly as I introduced myself.

"I know who you are," he grunted. And then, as though disinclined, "I'm Ossie."

Silence descended as my initial exuberance faded. Welcome to Spennymoor, I thought.

"Nice morning", I suggested gazing up at the brightening sky.

"Aye! Not bad for a Monday."

I was pleased when Dacre Long, PE'D and office keyholder, came along. He and I exchanged handshakes and pleasant introductions before he unlocked the door for the three of us to go inside. While Ossie opened a further set of doors to the rear yard, through which the morning's mail and the other postmen would arrive, Dacre invited me into his locker (GPO speak for secured office) and made me welcome. He explained that every morning, on a three week rotation, one of three drivers attended for duty at 4am to unlock the rear gates, drive an OMG (Official Motor Vehicle) to Bishop Auckland Delivery Office, an easy five miles away and return with bags of mail. From the delivery office in Bishop Auckland it was a short drive to the railway station to receive the final mail bags arriving from Darlington and then return to Spennymoor in time to re-open the gates for the others to start at 5pm. I was to be one of the three. Following inward sorting I would deliver mail to farms and rural communities culminating in Page Bank by the river Wear and south of Brancepeth Castle. Dacre then explained that my other two weeks would be, in turn, a walking delivery from Binchester Moor, taking in one of half of Middlestone Moor and finishing at the secondary school on Whitworth Lane. The third week was a split shift delivering mail in the Ox Close Crescent area and finishing at 10am. I was to report for the second part of the shift at 2:30pm and after a collection run through Byers Green and Binchester, take all of the day's earlier collections to Bishop Auckland for onward despatch to Darlington.

George Lavery accompanied me on my first three days. He remained by my side as I slowly got to grips with the inward sorting of the letters and packets for my Middlestone Moor delivery. He was most helpful and patient and we got along well. George was the other driver who, along with

Stan Bakewell, I would be joining on the three week rota. During inward sorting the union's Branch Secretary, Mark Dodd, introduced himself to me. We arranged to have a chat during the meal relief which formed the break between first and second deliveries.

I hadn't been at Spennymoor more than a couple of weeks when I observed animosity between Mark Dodd and Dacre Long. National agreements between the UPW and GPO afforded the recognition that, when acting in an official capacity, Branch Secretaries had equal status with whom they negotiated. But here in Spennymoor, neither man could stand the presence of the other. To put it prosaically one would endure no superior and the other would have no equal. Dacre, with the tacit support of the quisling Ossie Brown, who fancied himself as more PE status than PHG, would deliberately withhold operational information from Mark who in turn, invariably refused to agree to anything placed before him. Interminable union branch meetings were held where we were encouraged by Mark to reject changes to a duty, alterations to driving routes and a host of other issues. Disagreements, following open hostility and arguments between the two, frequently led to the intervention of the union's District Organiser, Darlington's Branch Secretary, Joe O'Rourke. Joe's experience and knowledge of the GPO, working practices and union rules would eventually lead to a settlement of sorts with one side or the other claiming a fragile victory.

Mark Dodd, a decent enough man, had our interests at heart as did, in many ways, Dacre Long and both believed they were doing the right thing for us in whatever argument beset them. It was a sad day then, when following a particularly vicious vocal exchange, Mark became unwell and had to go on sick leave. He was subsequently diagnosed as suffering from stress and he never returned to the office. Following a period of recovery he resigned and found a job as a bus driver.

During Mark's tenure, Carole and I married on Valentine's Day 1976. The ceremony took place in Spennymoor's St.Andrew's Church under the auspices of the Rev.Neville Baker, vicar and family friend of Carole and her mother. It was a sunny day and pleasantly warm and I stood resplendent in cream suit, matching waistcoat and flared trousers atop of brown platform soled shoes, the height of fashion at the time. I had a beard, save for a razor width from chin to lip and sported thick shoulder length hair. Standing outside the church with my brother Andy as my Best Man and with guests arriving, I was surprised when a Morris Oxford GPO van rolled up and out stepped Mark Dodd. He was grinning widely and as he approached I asked him what he was doing here.

"We've come to rescue you", he laughed.

Three of my other colleagues then sprung from the van, Alan Mattimoe, Barry Davison and Tommy Handley. To the laughter of Andy and the guests the four men bundled me into the rear of the van among piles of empty mail sacks and drove off. Of course, I was quickly returned unscathed and deposited back at the church but with dust and other detritus on my once pristine suit. The fun filled incident proved to be the highlight of the wedding just as my later marriage would prove to be unfulfilling and unhappy.

Although I no longer performed semi professionally, my music and songwriting meant a lot to me. I played at family gatherings and always took a guitar with me wherever I travelled on the off chance that I'd find a place to perform and someone willing to listen. During my time in Spennymoor I formed a Friday afternoon musical relationship with fellow postman, Alan Hardy. Alan was slightly older than me, well read, something of a poet and through him I was introduced to a wide range of music I had not previously listened to – Neil Young, Patty Smith, John Coltrane, Richard Thompson, Little Feat, The Third Ear Band to give an example of the diversity. In Alan's house, his mother out most Friday afternoons, we would listen to his vast record collection and play guitar to and with each other. I learned a lot from those sessions and, in later years when I returned to playing, I carried a lot of those new found influences with me.

I smoked my first joint in Alan's house. The experience wasn't pleasant as I had also drunk more than a few glasses of cheap white wine. I began to feel unwell and excused myself to stagger upstairs to the bathroom. The carpet rose up to meet me with each step and I collapsed on the bathroom floor momentarily losing consciousness. I came round with the room spinning and I felt like I wanted to be sick. As with many young men and women I had already experienced 'the spins' when drinking alcohol. It's almost a rite of passage and is eventually overcome with age and experience. But that afternoon, white wine and cannabis took me on a spin like I'd never had before nor hope to experience ever again.

Alan found me on the floor moaning incoherently and clutching the lavatory bowl. Whooooaa!! Not nice at all. That was definitely a lesson learned; alcohol *or* cannabis in future! Never, *ever*, mix the two. As a matter of fact I haven't smoked the stuff for over thirty years. Well, not regularly.

The office needed a new union Branch Secretary and I was conscious that my name was being mooted. At the annual meeting in February 1977 I had assumed the role of Treasurer. This fairly innocuous position afforded me access as a branch officer along with Mark and our Branch

Chairman, Alan Mattimoe, who was to later resign following Mark's departure, to some of the major and confidential matters overarching the branch and its members. Three of the most senior postmen, Tommy Handley, Arthur Spencely and Jack Attley cornered me during a meal relief and asked me to put my name forward. They told me that nobody else wanted to take on the role and that they had contacted Joe O'Rourke for advice. Joe had warned them that without a Secretary the branch might have to fold and be subsumed into Bishop Auckland or the colossus which was the mighty Darlington branch of the UPW. I took a few days to consider what I ought to do while fielding relentless encouragement from a number of my colleagues. Even Dacre Long said I should take on the role and in due course I agreed... but with a demand. I wanted Tommy Handley as Branch Chairman. Tommy accepted this largely organisational role astutely realising that what I was really after was a right hand man, and an experienced one at that. We were both elected unopposed.

There was much for me learn and I had to learn quickly. Back then there was no formal training for union officials as there is today but by attending meetings alongside Joe and my counterparts from other branches, I soon picked up the important fundamentals. In turn, at monthly meetings in Darlington between senior management and our district officers, I familiarised myself with processes and procedures, rules and regulations and matters pertaining to the wider operation. It was Joe who, during a break at one meeting, quietly advised me to, *'get to know the Head Postmasters Manual better than management do'.*

"Just watch me when we go back in," he said.

The meeting resumed and we came to a point of contention, the subject of which I can't recall, but things certainly weren't going our way. Joe stepped in and producing an A4 sheet of paper from his briefcase, began to read chapter and verse about why such a proposal could not be agreed and that, in his view, an impasse had been reached requiring national intervention. I watched as senior PE'B's, along with Darlington's Head Postmaster, Charles Woollage, looked at each other speechless weighing up the gravity of what Joe had read out. Not much else was said except for mutually agreeing to pass the matter up the chain and reconvene when necessary. With that we left and I stopped Joe on the loading bay as we made our way to the car park.

"Where the hell did you dig that ruling from?" I asked.

Joe winked and said that as we were losing the argument he had needed to stall for time. He then showed me the A4 sheet of paper... it was totally blank. The wily bugger had made it all up.

My role in disciplinary cases and local office based issues were dealt with using the Head Postmasters Manual and sage wisdom and advice from the likes of Joe and other senior union officers. On top of the aforementioned demands on my time there was a monthly all day meeting where postal branch officials met with our counterparts in British Telecom and Post Office Counters. And then there was the union's annual conference. As it is today, conference is first and foremost the union's sovereign body where, through a series of debates, industrial and political policies are formulated. Aside from its importance as a policy making body, annual conference determines lifelong friendships. There are some who I met at my first conference in Bournemouth 1978 with whom I maintain contact today.

Delegate numbers are greatly reduced now but back then two thousand or more UPW branch officials would converge from all parts of the UK for a 9am till 6pm, Sunday morning to Friday evening series of motions, amendments, debates, arguments, points of order, votes, exhibitions and fringe meetings. Compared to what was then a forty three hour a week job as a postman, annual conference required a weekly shift of some fifty four hours as well as regional delegate and divisional committee meetings most evenings. I was intrigued to note that some delegates clearly took advantage of the week away as an excuse for a holiday and contributing little or nothing to the actual business of conference. It was the same year after year. Now I am not suggesting that time out from such a relentlessly busy programme isn't important. It absolutely is. Indeed I made sure in my later years as a branch secretary, heading up the Darlington delegation, that we each had at least one day off during the week.

Yet in spite of the 'holidaymakers' the union remains overwhelmingly served by men and women of integrity who have only the interests of their members and the wider union at heart. They are by far the majority and ordinary members, many of whom have no particular interest in the work which goes on inside the union on their behalf, can be rightly proud of those who serve them.

So now I stood on the first rungs of a ladder which would take me on to a number of trade union positions over the course of the next thirty one years. Notwithstanding the workload, I was enjoying my union activities. Nevertheless, the steady schedule of meetings, grievances, disciplinary cases and what have you, none of which attracted a wage save for travel and subsistence, on top of having to do my job as a postman, began to take its toll on my ability to get up for work on time. Some days I'd get up for work at half past four, work a full shift and then head to a meeting which might, with travel included, not finish till after eight or nine at night. It wasn't long before I suffered the embarrassment of being knocked up at half past five in the morning. At first I managed to keep my 'lates' under control but over time they reached the point where I received my first warning letter. My embarrassment was made all the worse being handed the letter by the smug and grinning Supervising

PHG, Ossie Brown. Ossie and I had grown to distrust each other, he more so than I and he seemed to revel in any mishap I endured. I always felt that Ossie surreptitiously monitored my every move to take advantage of any and all opportunities to undermine or discredit me. Everybody has an *Ossie* at some point in their working life.

Delivery Offices had a Patrol Officer back then. The routes and timing of walks in those days was determined by a series of manually executed tests where, every now and then, postmen and women would be accompanied throughout their shift by an Operations Section employee from Darlington replete with clipboard and stopwatch noting how long it took to sort the mail and then how long it took to actually deliver it. Critical points on delivery were recorded. For example, arriving at the end of a street might be scheduled for say, 7:45am, emptying a post box as one passed by might be 8:15 etc etc. All this was methodically timed and logged for each duty. Patrol Officers were then allocated a specific daily delivery to check, ostensibly to comply with security regulations that stated where a postman or women ought to be at any given time. Ten minutes beyond the stated time triggered three suppositions... either the postman or woman was early and had already passed, that he or she was late, perhaps due to higher volumes of mail that day, or that an incident might have occurred somewhere on the route. Nowadays, this palaver of timing and recording deliveries is carried out by some clerical wonk beavering away at a computer who, in all likelihood, has no personal or operational knowledge of the location being tested.

A significant number of postmen and women have what are known as 'tea calls', places where members of the public and business owners provide a welcome cuppa. Whilst this unofficial break on a delivery is widespread, it is a practice that, in my day, was not permitted and would often lead to disciplinary action if caught. One of my tea calls was The Masons Arms pub on the main road through Middlestone Moor. My second delivery of the day was carried out on a bicycle and landlord, Alan Goad, former Hartlepool United footballer, welcomed me bringing my bicycle into his pub and parking it inside the entrance. This provided the dual advantage of preventing the bike being left unattended outside and, more importantly, it could not be seen by Ossie if he was on patrol. My free daily pint every three weeks went undetected until one fateful day I bade goodbye to Alan and wheeled the bike out on to the street just as Ossie was pulling up in his van. I was well and truly scuppered. Ossie was overjoyed. The eventual discipline hearing concluded with me being given a written warning to be placed on my record for six months.

There was yet to come another fateful day, one which was to have far reaching consequences and which almost cost me my job. I was on the 4am start to collect the mail from Bishop Auckland and return in time to open the gates for the 5am duties. I slept in. As I was scheduled to be the first to arrive at the office it meant that nobody would know I was late until they turned up to find the gates securely locked. I was the yard key holder and I was still in bed.

The knock on effect was dreadful. First, someone was dispatched in their own car to get me up. I then had to get to the office, open the gates to let in my none too pleased colleagues and then set off for Bishop Auckland. This meant, of course, that the mail which was due to arrive for inward sorting was delayed till around 6.30 with the subsequent further delay in getting people out on the streets to start their deliveries. I was not popular that morning, I can tell you. Later, when Ossie handed me the official sealed envelope containing the letter inviting me to a disciplinary interview, I wasn't at all surprised. It irked me, however, knowing that he knew what was in it; his smug grin said it all. In short, following a grovelling apology of a hearing, I was given a further written warning which stated that I had failed to maintain the necessary standards required and that should I be late by more than five minutes, twice in the following six months, I would be summarily dismissed. A bit strong, I thought. But I had no defence and I knew the chances of a successful appeal were minimal given that I already had a previous warning on my record. Even Joe O'Rourke representing me could only strive to ensure that the due processes were properly followed and applied. I vowed to up my game and save my job. It didn't last, however. Before a further three months had passed I slept in twice more.

On the day of my second oversleeping I was on the split shift doing afternoon collections. My route took me to the diminutive rural community of Byers Green where I was to empty a post box at the bottom of the village and then drive to the sub Post Office on the High Street to pick up letters, packets, parcels and, in those days but a practise long since ceased, sealed bags of money containing unknown amounts but reckoned by most to be hundreds if not several thousands of pounds.

"Hi, Sybil," I said as I went in. "Much for us today?"

The postmistress was a friendly soul and always ready to offer a cup of coffee and a chat.

"Hello, Phil," she replied without her usual pleasantness.

"What's up? Are you okay?" I asked.

"Is there a yellow car down the street? Did you pass one on the way up?"

"I don't know. I'll have a look. Why? What's the matter?"

Sybil didn't respond as I carried two or three bags of mail out to the van. I looked down the street and sure enough there was a yellow Vauxhall Chevette parked about one hundred yards away.

"It's been there for over an hour," said Sybil when I returned. "There's four men in it and every now and then one of them comes in and buys some stamps or cigarettes or chewing gum."

Charlie Horner, who I knew as a kindly pensioner who lived in the village was in the shop refusing to leave Sybil on her own until I had arrived.

"I reckon they're up to summat," he said.

"Really?"

At that moment the shop door opened and a young man with a teddy boy hairstyle, blue jeans and maroon corduroy jacket came in. I noticed Sybil stiffen.

"A packet of twenty Embassy Regal, love."

Sybil handed him the cigarettes and she looked at me as he was leaving the shop giving a nervous nod in his direction. I now understood something wasn't right.

"That's one of them", she said, her voice faltering. "He's been in before for some stamps about twenty minutes ago."

"Look, pet", said Charlie. "Now that Phil's here I'll be off. Watch yourself, mind."

Charlie left and I suggested that there was probably nothing of concern but that she should telephone the police just to be on the safe side. After making the call she told me the police were on their way but would I mind waiting in the shop till they arrived? We passed the time chatting until we were close to the point where I'd be late getting back with the collections. I was in enough trouble that day as it was.

"Sybil. I really must be getting on. The police are on their way and it's probably nothing to worry about. I'll give you a call when I get back to the office."

"Alright. But I'm going to lock the door when you've gone."

"Good idea. I'll call you in a bit."

I left a visibly concerned Sybil and climbed into the van, secured the doors, and set off while keeping an eye on the yellow Vauxhall in my mirrors. I didn't know what to think when the car set off too and I was pleased Sybil had shut the shop after I left. Except the car didn't stop at the Post Office. It kept on coming, getting closer and closer as the village street gave way to open countryside. Whoever was in the car were coming for me.

I'd always said that if ever there was an attempt to steal the mail I would not resist and would simply hand over whatever the robbers were after. It was a self preservation view shared by many of my colleagues. But right now, here I was facing that very threat and all I could think of was to get away. In no time at all the car was right on my tail, flashing its lights and horn beeping. I was absolutely scared stiff. My van's top speed was far too slow to outrun a family saloon. Thankfully, the narrow rural road consisted of a series of twists and turns and tight bends thus preventing my pursuers

67

from overtaking and cutting me off. With my foot hard down on the pedal I was in a state of heightened panic as I drove recklessly towards the junction with the C96 road which runs between Binchester and Newfield. So frightened was I and with my senses sharpened, I decided I would not slow down for the junction. Hoping that nothing would be coming from my right I would take the left hand turn at full speed and hope for the best. I felt it was my only hope, albeit a temporary one, as slowing down or stopping would have me trapped in whatever fate would befall. As I approached the junction I gritted my teeth and without taking my foot off the accelerator sped straight through and turned sharp left, centrifugal forces pushing my soft suspensioned Comma van to its limits. There was nothing coming from either right nor left. Thankfully.

My thoughts were focussed on getting to the next village, Binchester, and to find refuge there in the sub post office. The C96 straightened and my pursuers attempted to get alongside. My fear increased immeasurably and I felt I was done for. But then, at the very moment they had come alongside, gesticulating menacingly for me to pull over, I saw in the near distance a police car with blue lights flashing. My pursuers must have seen it as well because they slowed down and got back in behind me. As the speeding police car came in to view I flashed my lights and gesticulated frantically as we drew close. I swung the van off the main road into Binchester and saw in the mirrors that my pursuers were no longer behind me and were now fleeing towards the nearby A688 road which runs between Bishop Auckland and Durham. The police car had swung around too and I saw it give chase.

Once inside the safe haven of the sub Post Office I garbled my panic and fear to the postmistress who was incredulous at what I was telling her. My sense of relief from being safe was plain to see and I was shaking like a leaf and wanted to be sick. The postmistress handed me a cup of coffee while I used her telephone to contact the main GPO in Darlington where my call was put through to the Acting Head Postmaster, Jim Cotton-Betteridge, who later in his career would become Royal Mail's International Sales & Marketing Director. I explained to him what had happened, that there had been an attempt to rob the mail, that as far as I knew a police chase was in operation, and yes, the bloody mail was safe! He sensed how shaken I was and advised me to stay put and that he would personally arrange for someone to come out and take over my duty. I was then to be taken home and await further contact.

A police detective and Maurice Milner from the GPO Investigation Branch (IB) arrived at my home within minutes of each other just after 6pm. I was still quite shaken and after giving an account of the afternoon's events I was advised that I would need to make an official statement to

69

the police, probably the following day, and another to IB whenever a time could be allocated. The police officer then informed me that the men had indeed intended carrying out a robbery of the mail and the bags of money I was carrying and that they had been arrested following a pursuit to Durham City. I was shocked to be told that three of them were from a larger gang based in south London with 'friends' in Middlesbrough and they had been wanted by the police for some time. In addition, earlier in the day, these same four men had robbed the sub post office on Newgate Street in Bishop Auckland. I had to ask...

"Was I in any danger, myself?"

"Well," he said, "the one who came into the Post Office while you were there was local to the region and was probably sizing you up ahead of the attempt and, yes, they were equipped to use violence if necessary."

For the next few days I was shadowed by an unmarked police car wherever I went at work. I was informed that there was a considered risk that my subsequent appearance in court as a witness might, shall we say, be compromised by as yet unknown associates of the gang. I was also advised on personal security whilst at home and outside. Bloody hell!

As it turned out nothing further did happen but it took five or six weeks before I was fully confident at work again. During that time a preliminary hearing was scheduled at Bishop Auckland Magistrate's Court, ostensibly so that

Sybil, Charlie and myself could identify the men without having to undergo a formal identity parade. Inevitably, as well as having two policemen accompany the three of us, there were also members of the arrested mens' families in court too. I overheard one woman declaring to three others, *"that's the postman, and that's her who runs the post office, and that's that old bloke who kept walking past"*. It was all very concerning.

But what of my late attendances and summary dismissal? I think, perhaps, that because of what had happened there was a respectful delay in issuing the notice of my sacking. I recall it word for word...

Dear Mr.Graham

You are advised that due to you sleeping in a further two times in a six month period you have failed to demonstrate the standards required. You are therefore summarily dismissed.

However, owing to your recent actions in safeguarding Her Majesty's mail, we are prepared to reinstate you without loss of service. Should you accept the reinstatement a warning will be placed on your record for a period of twelve months during which time any failure to meet the standards required may result in your dismissal.

So. Sacked and reinstated in the same day! I didn't sleep in again.

4 – Darlington

Cliff Johnson, Spennymoor's PE'C, informed me that PHG training courses were available and that I should apply to go on one. I'd come to know Cliff, or CJ as we referred to him, not only as the delivery office PE'C but also through my branch official role. When Dacre and I exhausted whatever industrial or personnel issues lay before us, it was Cliff and Joe O'Rourke to whom the matter would be referred. After due consideration of the impasse and an examination of the issues, Cliff and Joe would pass the matter back to us with a solution or suggestions for further consideration.

To be honest I rather fancied the idea of becoming a PHG so I asked Cliff for an application form and sent it off. The course, lasting two weeks, took place in Harrogate and I was released from duty with full pay for the duration. Accommodation and travel expenses were provided along with a daily allowance. In addition, and this is where I paused to fully consider the implications, if successful I would be required to transfer to the main Darlington Delivery Office some sixteen miles away, itself scheduled for closure upon the opening of a new state of the art, high tech, MLO, or Mechanised Letter Office. Perhaps this was what was exercising CJ's mind; offload me and my trade union obstacles to someone else? Ha, ha. Perhaps I flatter myself.

Cliff Johnson was a decent yet simple man. He found it hard to grasp most things beyond the familiar and mundane. Once, for example, I wrote him a note about some issue on which he needed to be kept informed. I folded the note into an envelope and endorsed the cover, "FAO: Mr.C.Johnson" and left it on his desk. By mid afternoon I had been called to his office to explain why I was being so rude. Eh? What the hell was he referring to? I had to laugh when I found out that he had not understood that FAO were initials meaning *For the Attention Of* and that he was convinced the F stood for *Fuck* and that the O was *Off*. I can't recall what our conversation regarding the A led to.

I was pleased I decided to apply for the PHG course. Three further considerations helped form my decision; PHG's were paid more than postmen and women, PHG's worked indoors and, finally, I felt the newness of both job and workplace were an attractive proposition; a new start after the trouble I had been in.

Harrogate's Adelphi Hotel on Cold Bath Road is where I checked in on Monday 10th April 1978. I arrived in plenty of time for the start of the course at 1pm a short drive away on a campus shared with other public sector industries. Security checked, signed in and accredited, I joined five others to be introduced to our tutor, Eddie Jennings. Eddie had a smile and personality to calm even the most nervous student. It wasn't long then before we were all relaxed and confidently going through the ritual of introducing ourselves, stating where we had come from, married or otherwise and what our interests were.

The duties of a PHG are extensive and much too varied to list here. But fundamentally, working primarily in caged, secured lockers, PHG's, apart from a higher knowledge of sorting destinations, were responsible for the receiving, handling and despatching of sealed bags of cash, high value items and, of course, registered mail. From and to each shift were passed paper closing balances indicating what was being transferred to the next stage. There was no room for error. The importance of our tasks and the implications for mistakes were drilled home at every stage throughout the course. One piece of light advice from Eddie was, *"stamp everything, initial everything and you won't go far wrong!"* Any item leaving an office via a PHG locker had a paper trail right through to its final office of destination and ultimate delivery. In that way, anything which went missing could be easily traced to a particular point in the process for investigation and hopeful recovery. Compensation for delay or loss costs the Post Office a fair bit of money each year.

I waited to hear if my time on the training course had been a success. I had a feeling that it had from the positive feedback I received from Eddie and when Cliff called me in to present me with the good news, I was delighted. I set about making arrangements for my successor as the call to transfer to Darlington could come in a few days or a few weeks. There was no way of knowing so I wanted to make sure that someone was in place to take over my role as Branch Secretary or, at the very least, to ensure Tommy could carry on in proxy if not.

My parting farewell was to Ossie Brown. I knocked at his locker door and went in without waiting to be admitted.

"Ossie", I said. "Fair play to you, mate. But, remember this...I shall be around at your downfall."

He just laughed, blew a fart and turned away.

Darlington Delivery Office was a three storey, red brick, grade 2 listed building which I found hugely imposing compared to the rudimentary office I had just left. Operating around the clock in Crown Street the ground floor, with its access to vehicular loading and unloading bays, was where mail was received and from whence it was despatched to all parts of the UK. Mail arrived for sorting via collections from post boxes, OMV's (Official Motor Vehicles) and TPO's (Travelling Post Offices) - the mail trains which passed through Darlington between London and Scotland. On the second floor were the inward and outward sorting areas from where the town and its rural communities were delivered. Along a rear wall was a line of PHG lockers. The upper floor was where the union office and the secretive Investigation Branch were located along with a restroom where meal reliefs were taken. Charles Woollage, the rotund and balding area head postmaster with whom I had frequently crossed swords as branch secretary in Spennymoor, passed me on the stairs from the restroom.

"Ah. I heard I had another bolshie in the office!" he sneered.

Charming.

The union structure in Darlington was massive in comparison to my two previous workplaces. Alongside Branch Secretary Joe O'Rourke was his chairman, the avuncular Don Ross who, rather than adopt a purely administrative role that I was used to, was instead positively active in the branch affairs. Joe and Don were supported by a Branch Treasurer, an Indoor Section Secretary, an Outdoor Section Secretary, a Night Shift Secretary, a Counters Secretary and a powerful and influential committee. Understandably, being the new kid in town, I had no union role to play nor would I until a couple of years later when we relocated to a new, highly automated, Mechanised Letter Office on St.Cuthberts Way. From there Joe would eventually retire, Don would transfer to Northallerton and new officials would take over. I did however attend union meetings voicing my opinion where appropriate and voting accordingly.

As a PHG in Crown Street I was consigned to work in the registered lockers as part of a four man rotation which included Claude Gooch, Ken Bainbridge and Dave

Charlesworth. Dave went on, some years later, to be the DOM in Barnard Castle and I held him in some regard in that later post for his steady hand and care for his staff. Dave and I maintained contact after our respective retirements, although I prefer to use the term 'retread' and I was sad to hear of his death from cancer in March 2019.

Work on constructing the Mechanised Letter Office, a vast brick building with corrugated roof, commenced in 1981 and was officially opened in 1982 by the Duke of Gloucester. By then my photography hobby was, pardon the pun, developing. In this I shared a joint enterprise with Ed Spence, a fellow amateur photographer and near neighbour in Tudhoe Colliery. We were known by our initials – P & E Photography. Ed had media connections as a trackside marshall at many of the country's motorcycling circuits and in August 1978 he invited me to Cadwell Park in Lincolnshire for the prestigious event, "The Bill Ivy Trophy". Introducing me to the clerk of the course Ed got me signed on as a press photographer with a coveted Access All Areas pass. I promised the clerk of the course some photos by way of appreciation and was surprised and delighted in equal measure when one of my shots was used for the front cover of the following season's programme. I was even more delighted when a royalties cheque arrived in the post. It was the start of a reasonably lucrative sideline career travelling with Ed to photograph weekend motorcycle events at Cadwell, Snetterton, Scarborough, Croft and the world superbike grand prix at Donnington Park. Heady times, indeed. My lenses captured stills and action shots of the likes of world champion rider Barry Sheene along with Randy Mamola, Mick Grant, Steve Parrish and the UK's up and coming hero, 'Rocket' Ron Haslam.

Of course, the really useful money came from many local commissions photographing weddings, family portraits and community events. My first wedding shoot, incidentally, came about as a complete fluke. I was ready to go Saturday afternoon shopping with Carole when the phone rang.

"Hi, Phil. It's Ed. What are you doing this afternoon?"

"Erm, nothing much apart from shopping. Why?"

"I'm at a wedding in Spennymoor and the photographer hasn't turned up. I've told the bride and groom I'd get you to come along and take some pics."

"You're fucking joking!" I spluttered. "I've never done a wedding in my life."

"I know", Ed acknowledged. "Just some snaps will be fine. Come on. We're all relying on you, Phil."

At least the call got me out of the shopping trip as Carole gave me her grudging approval to attend the wedding. Within an hour I was introduced to the bride and groom and with absolutely no previous wedding photography experience, got down to work. How I got through the next few hours was down to a thorough knowledge of my cameras and equipment, an understanding of light and shadow plus my long established eye for composition. I delivered a series of 6" x 4" prints to the newlyweds a week later and they were overjoyed with what they saw. Even I had to admit that my efforts hadn't been at all bad. However, it must also be said that what I went on to produce over the next thirty years was far superior to my first nervous and unskilled effort on that day.

"Thank you", said the husband. "You got us out of a mess here. Will this be alright?" He handed me eighty pounds. "If that's not enough just say."

"No. No. It's okay. Really. I did this for my friend, Ed.

"Well, take it with our compliments. Well be in touch soon for some reprints and enlargements."

Driving home I pondered this stroke of financial good fortune. I hadn't expected to be paid and with my postman wage of around thirty four pounds a week, eighty pounds felt like excessive largesse. I was delighted. So was Carole. From that moment on I studied many styles of wedding photography and embarked upon a fledgling career alongside my full time job with Royal Mail. It was a move that would impact positively on my earnings and business acumen many years later.

Hearing that the Duke of Gloucester was to open the Mail Centre and with my now established background as a serious amateur photographer, I was surprised to be denied access by Royal Mail chiefs to take some photos of the event alongside the invited press. I was knocked back at every turn with the only explanation given being *"security"*. What bollocks. I knew quite well that the refusal was more to do with that age old get-out that people use when it's easier to say "no" than being bothered to deal with issues. I also think another reason for the refusal was that they didn't want someone from the hoi polloi getting close to landed gentry. We, the uniformed plebs were kept well back while the suits and ties took centre stage.

It's a fact of life, this inability by some in authority to acquiesce to unexpected requests. It starts in school and continues throughout life. And whereas it isn't always possible to change closed minds, my advice is to always challenge the buggers to justify saying "no". It's surprising how they squirm with embarrassment or become annoyed and wish you'd just leave them alone. Sometimes, though, with a bit of persistence, a closed mind actually opens enough to say 'yes'. Betty Hardisty, my former English teacher, understood this and told me so. Betty was ahead of the game.

Whilst retaining traditional deliveries there was now the addition of a Processing Centre and a Distribution Centre under the same roof and the service was divided into three clear and distinct operations. The delivery operation is self explanatory and, as one would expect, the Distribution Centre handled the receipt of afternoon and evening collections and distributed the mail which had been processed during the day. Processing the mail is precisely that but with the vast bulk of inward and outward sorting now automated through coding desks where, seated at noisy clattering consoles with an eye level moving belt conveying letters from right to left, suitably trained PHG's would read an address or postcode, type the details and thereby infuse the passing envelope with a 'code' of blue phosphor dots. Once coded the letters were then conveyed by more belts to an Automated Sorted Machine (ASM) where the phosphor dots would be read and translated under ultra violet light and automatically directed to one of a hundred and forty four destination boxes.

By 1977 I wanted to set up a new band. Memories of playing bass in Victoria were never far from my mind and I'd heard that a couple of young fellas near to where I lived were looking for an outfit to join. I tracked them down to Low Spennymoor Club where they rehearsed on Monday evenings. Kevin Bowtell played drums and his friend, Mick McGough, played guitar. I was twenty seven and these two were teenagers. Yet in spite of the age difference, we got on well and agreed to get together and run through some songs with Mick and myself sharing the vocals. With my previous experience and their command of contemporary chart songs our repertoire was impressive and rehearsals went well. Neither of them had played in public so I needed to get them blooded somewhere friendly and where they could get a feel for what I hoped was to come later... weekend touring. I contacted a friend, Albert Hauxwell, who arranged for us to play in his local club in the nearby village of Newfield. With that in the diary we jointly purchased an HH PA system from Hamilton's, a popular music store in Middlesbrough, and set about working up a set of songs suitable for our debut.

We called ourselves Panther and knocked out popular tunes from the time. For a three piece we sounded okay. What I hadn't reckoned on, though, was first night nerves and come the day of the gig Mick had major doubts about his readiness and ability for the evening's show. He was on edge all day and feeling generally unsettled. I was relieved to see that he seemed to have calmed down by the time we arrived at the venue and I kept things light hearted as we set up the stage with people coming in and taking their seats. I was well known in Newfield so the banter between the swelling crowd and the three of us was good natured as we prepared for the show. I thought that had helped to calm Mick's nerves. Wrong.

We had a male vocalist on the bill that night who was to start off the evening's entertainment and with bingo to follow it would be a couple of hours before we went on. I suggested to the boys that they should relax and go out, have a walk around and come back at nine o'clock. So what did they do? They went straight over the road to the Queen's Head pub where Mick, I suspect on an empty stomach, got drunk. I could tell he was unstable when he came back to the club. Kevin had had a few but Mick was beyond help. He could barely stand. This debut for Panther was in jeopardy unless Mick could contain himself for two half hour sets.

The first mishap occurred stepping on to the stage when Mick stumbled headlong and downwards into Kevin's drums. Above the noise of cursing and crashing cymbals I heard laughter from some in the crowd who thought it was part of the act. What a shock they were going to get. Kevin and I got our unsteady guitarist to his feet and stood him in front of a mic ready for the first song. He missed his cue altogether. I have a rule which, with the exception of dire circumstance, does not permit songs to be restarted once they have begun. If anyone misses a cue or is late coming in, I expect the others to keep on playing and eventually all will kick back into place. Well, Mick did find his way in and we got the first song over to polite but hardly enthusiastic applause. I introduced our next song explaining that this was the first time Mick and Kevin had appeared in public. That garnered a bit of sympathy and understanding for a while but the next few songs can only be described as average and when we left the stage at the break I was fucking livid.

Our second set had hardly begun when Mick, having had a couple of more drinks in the break, stumbled forward knocking over his mic stand into the front row. Drinks were spilled and people were more than a bit miffed. I could see that Mick was beyond sobriety so I did something I had never done before and hope never to do again... I stopped the show, apologised to the audience and walked off.

That was the end of Panther and my damaged reputation in Newfield took months to repair. Admittedly, most people who were at the show knew it wasn't me who had caused the problem and over time hurtful derision turned to friendly laughter. Some years later I played a solo show in Newfield and regained my honour. Mick and I met again, quite by chance, forty two years later during a show I was doing in The Black Horse, Tudhoe. We were both delighted to see each other and reminisced and laughed about that fateful debut in Newfield.

Bereft of love in my marriage I became a bit of a wild card. Cocksure to the core and getting braver by the week. I took to making up excuses to attend non-existent trade union meetings which somehow went on later than usual. In fact I was becoming acquainted with a number of Spennymoor divorcees and single mothers through their social associations with my discreet sister in law, Janet Rowley, now living with her three children on the town's Bessemer Park Estate. Thus, Carole and I, loveless and directionless, split up by mutual consent with me leaving on Boxing Day 1982. I went back to Bishop Auckland to live with my brother who was also going through a divorce.

At that time Andy lived in a one bedroomed rented house at no.1 Edward Street, barely big enough for both of us and where I kipped in a sleeping bag in his living room. Our living arrangements were not satisfactory and by the middle of the following year we had moved to 3A Wharton Street in Coundon from where my own divorce proceedings commenced. 1983 was a pivotal year for me in a number of ways, not just for the anticipated divorce, but at the year's end I met Janet Jackson. Neither of us knew at the time that she would eventually leave where she lived and worked in Darwen near Blackburn to move in with myself and Andy. We bought our current house in New Coundon in September 1985, got married in December 1993 and raised two children becoming happy and proud grandparents in 2015 and 2019.

When Joe O'Rourke retired Mick Shields was elected to replace him. With Don Ross as chairman, section secretaries and committee, Mick was a significant force representing members' personal and collective interests and in industrial relations matters. However, where Joe had carried out his role through open dialogue and persuasion Mick, though sincere and dedicated but lacking his predecessor's wealth of wisdom, guile and experience, adopted a more demanding and slightly aggressive demeanour. Joe made friends to achieve his aims, Mick was more direct.

At the branch annual general meeting in January 1983 I was elected to serve on the committee. Through attending monthly meetings, it wasn't long before I began to feel confident playing my part alongside my committee colleagues acting as the eyes and ears of all that was going on. I attended that year's annual conference in Blackpool with a delegation large enough, including colleagues from Middlesbrough MLO and associated BT and Counters grades, to warrant the hiring of a coach. The number of delegates permitted to attend annual conference is determined by the number of members in a branch. As Branch Secretary in Spennymoor I had attended conference on my own and now here I was surrounded by a dozen or so others.

Upon our return a rumour had begun to circulate about a PHG who had been caught misappropriating an Official Motor Vehicle; a most serious offence indeed. When I found out that the PHG was Ossie Brown I resisted the urge to gloat and call him to offer representation at his subsequent disciplinary hearing where, if I remember correctly, he was awarded a serious offence to be kept on his records for a period of time. Not quite the downfall I had predicted when I had said goodbye to him, but I was never as mean spirited towards him as he had frequently been to me.

Don Ross transferred to Northallerton Delivery Office shortly after conference and Mick, too, moved away somewhere to the south of the country. The subsequent elections brought in the immensely popular and imposing John Hollingworth as branch secretary. The very epitome of larger than life, John possessed a tremendous sense of fun. He was also unreservedly loyal to the branch and its members. So highly regarded was he that during a heated exchange with a female operations section employee, she suspended him with immediate effect. Within moments of the suspension being known every postman, postwoman and PHG stopped work and walked out refusing to return until John had been reinstated. Hearing of the walkout, Head Postmaster John Ensoll, by nature a quiet, church going man, stormed into the car park where around a hundred or so of us had assembled in resolute defiance.

"What on earth is going on?" he demanded to know. "This is simply
ridiculous!"

Andy Caygill, the new branch chairman, tried to respond but his words were drowned out by collective chanting and jeering. Sensing the mood of defiance, John Ensoll invited a handful of committee members to come to his office and discuss the situation. Three or four of us volunteered to accompany Andy and, if my memory serves, assistant head postmaster Mike Binks and Harry Bennett, senior operations manager were present, too. We were initially subjected to an unnecessary rundown of the illegality of our action before our demands were sought and given. In short we said we would accept nothing less than the full reinstatement of our branch secretary and an apology from the woman who had suspended him.

Our demands were based on the premise that she had taken the easy route towards resolving the argument as opposed to actively seeking a resolution. Ensoll and his team, clearly anxious to get us back to work, offered us a full and frank review of the situation if we would immediately return to work. We reported back to our colleagues in the car park where the offer was universally rejected and we returned to Ensoll and his team to say so. After a further round of fractious deliberations we were given an undertaking that our demands would be met in so far as John would be reinstated without penalty but an apology would not be forthcoming.

We had secured a positive outcome and we agreed a set of terms which were drafted up in writing. The document, duly signed by John Ensoll and Andy Caygill, was presented to the increasingly impatient crowd waiting outside. I was feeling quite elated that a full blown dispute had been averted and had fully anticipated an orderly return to duty. I couldn't have been more wrong. John Hollingworth was quick to spot that the agreement made no reference to the fact that he would be reinstated 'immediately' nor, in fact, did it state any particular time.

"Fuck 'em", he said. "There's no apology so we'll go back in tomorrow!"

To rapturous applause and brutish cheers (there were some pretty hardline postmen and women in that car park) we promptly dispatched a note to John Ensoll, stood around till the end of our shifts and then went home. John received an apology by the end of the week. We all lost a days pay.

In time, John had us taking similar action in support of a young postman by the name of Colin Freeman who many of us felt had been unjustly treated over an on-delivery issue by a stressed out supervisor. When Colin was suspended, John had us all out of the building in a matter of minutes. More than one hundred trade union members stood defiantly outside until due process had been observed and justice seen to be done.

John was blunt but fair in everything he asked us to support. Although a renowned wit and joker, never once did he engage us in a dispute without the reasons and consequences having first been the subject of calm and reflective thought. Oh, how I wish I could have garnered such loyalty and support from members when I became branch secretary not too many years later.

Time moved steadily on and my role on the branch committee came to the attention not just of my work colleagues but also of our shift supervisors. Being somewhat outspoken I was often approached by members to make representations on their behalf. A number, particularly women, preferred this approach as opposed to calling on full blown union intervention. I was always careful, nonetheless, to report such matters back through the committee. I was beginning to establish a reputation as an advocate on behalf of union members and a bit of a pain in the backside of some supervisors who couldn't (or wouldn't) play fair.

Don Ross's transfer to Northallerton had triggered a spate of chairmen - they were always men, never women – in quick succession. Two of the most noteworthy in terms of their impact on myself are the aforementioned Andy Caygill and a personal friend of mine, Bill Oxbrough. Andy would hold the position for far longer than Bill and both became managers when the GPO later rebranded itself under the name Post Office Group.

Andy and I had been soulmates on many a union delegation at regional committee meetings, special conferences, national briefings and the like. In my view, though, Andy had a fundamental flaw; an abject lack of input at conferences where he was infinitely better suited to

91

the hectic evening rounds of socialising and networking where determinations on which way to vote and who to support or oppose in the following day's debates were often made. The trouble was that Andy did rather too much socialising and not enough networking. In the MLO he was second to none when representing the branch and its members but he was lightweight at conference never willing nor, I suspect, sufficiently capable of taking part in debates except for raising his hand and voting.

As the years drifted by we maintained a friendly working relationship and when I later became chairman he was both the branch secretary and area delivery representative, the latter being a new role brought about by the introduction in the mid nineteen nineties of The Industrial Relations Framework. It was regrettable then, undoubtedly due to the relentless demands and complexities of his dual roles, that Andy's focus and effectiveness began to wane. I started to receive complaints about his perceived lack of commitment to members, particularly where those working in outlying delivery offices were concerned.

His position became untenable after I challenged him about a phone call I had taken from Kath Kinnear, a postwoman in Northallerton telling me that Andy had not kept an appointment to assist her with a disciplinary matter she was facing. That had been one complaint too many and it had come on the same day that I received a motion of no confidence in him which was signed by over sixty members. Remaining supportive, yet failing to get him to explain to me what was going on, I asked him to consider his position. He was visibly taken aback by my suggestion and we had a difficult discussion in which he stressed that he was simply busy and refuted my assertion that members were being let down. In the end I asked him to resign one of his two union positions. He wouldn't hear of it so I advised him that I would convene a special branch committee meeting where I was obliged to have the motion of no confidence considered.

The case against Andy was presented to committee along with all supporting evidence. He exercised his right to respond offering nothing that hadn't already been noted. Committee members then asked questions and he gave his answers. When the vote was taken the motion of no confidence was carried to be put before a subsequent meeting of branch members with only Ian Pringle, the branch Treasurer, not voting and suggesting that perhaps we were being a bit harsh.

Andy Caygill was now no longer the area delivery representative, bar his right to appeal which he did not pursue. The carrying of the motion was no easy matter for me and I still had to work with Andy in his role as branch secretary. However, my mindset was such that friendships cannot be allowed to stand in the way of accountability.

I found out several weeks later that Andy had not wished any of us to know that he had been having quite overwhelming problems of a personal and domestic nature but did not wish to say what those problems were. Eventually he knew the game was up, left his wife and family and successfully applied to become a manager and transferred to Newbury.

Bill Oxbrough and I have enjoyed a personal and family friendship stretching back to the time when he arrived with the grand transfer from delivery offices to fill PHG vacancies in the new MLO. We enjoy similar tastes in music, our politics aren't too dissimilar and we have served together as councillors on Wear Valley District Council. In the intervening years we have confided in each other, played guitars together, walked the hills in all seasons, got drunk, been to concerts and, still today, our families exchange Christmas cards and gifts. In the beginning, though, we simply worked alongside each other manually sorting outward mail. A bit of a joker with a ready wit and developed intellect, Bill could either be the life and soul of the shift or earnestly serious. An illustration of the closeness I came to share with Bill is nicely illustrated with the following episode...

It was FA Cup Final day, Saturday 14th May 1994, featuring Manchester United and Chelsea. Bill and I had his house in Leeholme to ourselves while our wives, Julie and Janet, went out shopping. As men typically do on such occasions we consumed a fair few tins of beer prior to the match and onwards long after the kick off. During the half time break, suitably toileted and opening more tins, we turned to the subject of Bill's progress with a barbering course he had recently enrolled on. I was intrigued enough to ask if he had time to cut my hair before the second half started. Satisfied that he could we went out the back with a chair, towels, comb and scissors.

Remember, we had both drunk quite a bit and the second half was well underway before I began to question whether Bill's tonsorial prowess was best not practised while under the influence. I couldn't see of course, having no mirror, but Bill's frequent cursing with each snip, interspersed with tipsy, barely suppressed laughter convinced me things weren't right.

"How's it going, Bill?" I asked nervously.

"Not very well if I'm honest, heh, heh. I just need to er...*snip*... match up the other side a little bit more with er...*snip, snip*... heh, heh, this side."

"What? But you've already cut the other side!"

"I know. I know... heh, heh. I'll er... get it right in just a minute..."

At that moment the Julie and Janet arrived home from shopping and I knew straight away that something had gone horribly wrong. The look of on their faces was enough to get me off the seat and into the house to find a mirror. The reflection I saw could not have been worse. Bill had made a right balls of my locks with some bits longer than others and a spiky section to the left of my crown next to an almost bald patch on the right. Hair down left side on my neck was noticeably shorter than the right. What a sight. What a laugh. Yes, we laughed and laughed, the two of us now completely out of control. The more Julie laid verbally in to Bill and Janet scolded me the more hilarious the situation became.

Manchester won 4 – 0 by the way.

I wore a wool hat on the way to Blades on Monday morning, not taking it off until I was inside the salon. Jane, my usual stylist back then led the chorus of shock and surprise.

"Oh my god! What have you done?"

As Jane and her colleagues moved from disbelief to outright laugher I sheepishly explained the events of the previous Saturday afternoon.

"Get sat down and let's see what can be done", she giggled.

Jane performed miracles that morning. Unable to work without more drastic cutting and shaping she explained that I would be left with very short hair by the time she was finished. And by heaven she was right. For the next few weeks, instead of my usual collar length styling, I was reduced to what could only be described as an extreme crew cut. To this day Bill and I still laugh over that delightfully drunken episode. He did not go on to complete his barbering course.

Bill's role as branch chairman, working alongside John Hollingworth, came about while I was still a member of the committee. As a duo Bill and John were a match made in heaven. They shared a similar sense of humour and both men were able see through the froth of issues to what was fundamentally important. In time both went on to become Royal Mail managers. And although each would be employed across a variety of managerial roles, it is in Richmond delivery office where I best remember John and with Bill it is during his time in the same role at Spennymoor.

It was during this time, as branch secretary, the post I had been elected to following the departure of Andy Caygill, I no longer had any direct industrial relations input with delivery office managers although I was kept informed about issues by the union's workplace representatives. Accordingly, because my family and personal relationships with Bill were well known I had to remain distant and non-committal when reports came in of the issuing of disciplinary awards and a suspension from duty under his charge. It was important that the local rep and the Area Delivery Representative be left to deal with such matters while I was acutely conscious of the scrutiny I was under being Bill's friend. It was an uncomfortable time but I did not become involved or express any opinions. That didn't make me immune to the emotion, of course, but I simply noted the reports and trusted the reps to deal with things. Besides, there were other officers in the branch who could give advice and guidance as needed.

Two other managers on the scene at this time, one who started out as a postman like Bill and myself, were Mick Storey and Paul Jobling. These two were generally regarded throughout the area as rather unsavoury pieces of work in respect of the manner in which they treated their staff. Funnily enough I got on well with Mick when we worked together as PHG's but I saw a darker side of him when he ditched the uniform for a suit and tie. A confident and at times over-assured man he exuded an air unvalidated superiority, especially in meetings with senior managers and union officials. He would frequently turn up to meetings a few minutes late feigning a heavy schedule had delayed him. It was a game he played in order to be noticed but I don't think many were fooled.

Mick had long insisted that I should become a manager. In fact I did apply once and was accepted. I didn't last long, five or six weeks at the most, as I was totally unsuited to carrying out a role where I was expected by some, in particular our office PE'C at the time, John Leggett, to be hard on staff. I resigned after I was complicit, through instruction, in getting somebody sacked.

Anyway, prior to that unsavoury period, I received an invitation from Mick Storey to a dinner for managers in the Marriott Hotel in Newcastle upon Tyne. Mick advised that I would not be permitted to attend the daytime events but he would be delighted to later introduce me to some senior Royal Mail managers socially in the hope that I might consider relinquishing my trade union post and become *'one of them'*. After much persuasion I agreed to go along. Mike McGinley, one of Royal Mail's regional directors was there. He and I knew each other reasonably well and we shared a friendly and cordial working relationship. Mick Storey, bless him, wasn't aware of this and thought it would be good sport to introduce me to Mike, ply me with drink and see if he could get me drunk enough to open up about the union's plans on a range of issues and policies. His plot backfired as Mike and I talked about everything except work while enjoying the generosity of Mick's wine bill. Mick became slowly but surely drunk on his own vino largesse and, shuffling from the table, eventually staggered unsteadily away to bed.

Some months later, following an investigation into incidents which had allegedly taken place at a party held by managers celebrating their black-legging and scabbing during a legitimate and lawful trade union strike, Mick

99

Storey was sacked. As for Paul Jopling, a man who upon his appointment to Darlington disdainfully threw the Head Postmasters Manual in to a waste bin in the presence of Andy Caygill and myself, I was simply pleased when he eventually moved away altogether – a view shared by others.

Although I was receiving reports about the situation at Spennymoor the subject was never broached whenever Bill and I were together socially. Sadly, perhaps inevitably, we reached a point where the unspoken situation in Spennymoor became a strain on our relationship and we didn't speak to each other or meet for a year or so. It was a difficult time. Happily, though, our friendship recovered shortly after Bill's return to the MLO to work in Operations. Our families remain in contact.

There is a further noteworthy aside which I recall during this period. It relates to John Hollingworth and is one of many which more than adequately sums up his superior perceptiveness and sense of fun. In the years leading to the millennium, the union's area delivery representative was ex military policeman, John Mason, who worked at Richmond Delivery Office.

Scrupulously fair, bullish, if hopelessly naive at times, John Mason was driven solely by the interests of those he was elected to serve. He would display no weakness in the face of hostility or opposition, nor when those with whom he was negotiating had the upper hand. Standing firm against any and all who tried to outdo him, he was generally tolerated by managers rather than openly castigated for errors in argument or judgement. His members valued him highly. To be represented by John Mason was to know that no stone would be left unturned until he got the result which he felt was right. Many is the time myself or the union's regional secretary and divisional representatives had to get him to back away from applying for highly expensive and unwinnable industrial tribunals and from his frequent invocations of European Court Of Human Rights legislation. Naive he may well have been but nobody could question his unremitting service to his members.

It came as a surprise therefore when he called me at home late one evening. He had been summoned to appear before his manager, John Hollingworth, to answer a charge of alleged misconduct and, although more than capable of dealing with it himself, he said wanted to exercise his right to be represented.

"No problem, John", I said. "When is it?"

"In the morning. Half past five!"

"You're kidding, aren't you?"

"No, I'm not. I need you at half five!"

"But I haven't even seen the paperwork. Who are you up against?"

"Holly!"

"John Hollingworth! Bloody hell, John. He'll skin you alive."

"That's why I need you, Phil."

I arrived at Richmond delivery office at quarter to five the next morning and went immediately to the union office where my "client" was drinking tea. We had just enough time for a recap and a glance at the case papers and it was time to go in. I felt like requesting an adjournment for a later start.

"Does he know it's me who you've asked along?" I enquired.

"No. I haven't told him, yet."

"Well, this will be fun", I thought.

We walked determinedly to the delivery manager's office. John knocked twice and we went in. Holly's face was a picture the moment it dawned on him that not only did he have the most tenacious area delivery representative to discipline but the branch secretary would be representing him.

"Oh, fuckin' hell", he cried throwing his hands in the air in mock surrender. "I might as well give up now!"

And with that, slowly shaking his head and grinning from ear to ear, he drew the case papers out of the file, tore them in two and threw them in the bin. I was back home by six thirty. All charges dropped.

5 - Political Beginnings

Stepping back in time to July 1985 Janet and I had returned from a weekend trip to Belfast and Ballyclare with our friends Mark Everett, a postman colleague of mine, and his girlfriend, Barbara Harrison. It had been a rough return sea crossing followed by a long drive down from the ferry terminal at Cairnryan and we were all tired by the time we pulled up outside The Swamp – the name we had given to the home at 3A Wharton Street which Janet and I shared with my brother, Andy. We got back just after two o'clock in the morning and our friends accepted our invitation to stay the night and drive back to their home in Darlington the following day.

Mark helped me carry bags from the car while Janet went ahead with Barbara to open the front door. I didn't think anything unusual in that Andy's car wasn't parked in the street and my weary thoughts were of changing into comfortable clothes and relaxing with a late night cuppa. I dropped our bags just inside the entrance and stepped into the living room while Janet went into the kitchen to make hot drinks.

"Phil", she called.

"Yeh. What's up?"

"Come here, will you!? There's no cups!"

Sure enough, there were indeed no cups. There were no saucers or plates either and no bowls nor pans. Nor was there any cutlery save for my personal heirloom knife and fork. An electric kettle which belonged to our landlady was the only item, solitary upon the kitchen worktop.

"What the bloody hell....!" I exclaimed.

It was at that point that we noticed, too, most of the kitchen utensils were missing along with grocery stuff such as coffee, tea, bread and milk.

"Is everything okay in there?" Barbara called.

I left Janet looking through cupboards which, for the most part, were empty and went back in to where Mark and Barbara sat. I then saw that the stereo system and a rack of cassette tapes were missing along with several LP records. Had we been burgled? I went upstairs and quietly knocked on Andy's bedroom door. I knocked again, harder this time and receiving no response opened the door and went in. He wasn't in bed. Indeed, his bed had been stripped to the mattress and the wide open wardrobe doors showed there were no clothes hanging there. I had absolutely no idea what was going on. Mystery abounds.

In those days we did not have mobile phones so there was no way I could contact my brother directly. I decided against phoning the police and when everyone retired to bed I slept uneasily. Just after seven, deprived of sleep and unable to contain myself any longer, I telephoned my uncle Bobby in

Newton Aycliffe and asked if he knew where Andy was. Bobby, who my brother was especially close to and in whom he confided many things, was surprised to learn that I didn't know that Andy had moved out of The Swamp and into a flat in Newton Aycliffe. He explained that Andy had begun planning to move after Janet and I had recently announced that we were looking to buy a house of our own and he had been given the keys to his new flat the previous Friday – the day we had gone to Ireland. My brother had secretly moved out over the weekend while we were away, stripping The Swamp in the process. We laugh about it now but it was several weeks before Andy and I were back on speaking terms and by that time Janet and I had moved into our current home in New Coundon.

It was while living in Wharton Street that I had met Frank Webster, a man who would come to have a major influence on my further political thinking. Frank, then in his late sixties, had served with the Royal Navy during the second world war and later retired from service as a railway employee. He moved into Station House in New Coundon with his wife, Rose in 1954. Their home was the station masters house on the branch line between Bishop Auckland and Durham. Having opted for a simple later life, Frank spent his days tending extensive vegetable plots, rearing hens and taking frequent lengthy walks with his terrier dog,

Miffy. The two were often seen together on the myriad footpaths and rights of way which beset this delightful semi rural location. Renowned for championing local causes, Frank wrote copious carefully considered letters of objection and protest to local and national newspapers, district and county council officers and both large and small business organisations. He was especially welcomed at public meetings speaking for or against issues of local concern.

In contrast he never made a fuss of the fact that he had received the British Empire Medal for services to the public and community. He possessed a developed intellect and was especially well read; one room in Station House was given over to such classics by Fyodor Dostoevsky, Ernest Hemingway, Jane Austen, Leo Tolstoy, William Shakespeare and, of course, Charles Dickens from whose works Frank could quote without hesitation. Amongst these great literary tomes were dozens of lighter books by the likes of Spike Milligan, Harper Lee, Ogden Nash, Mark Twain and more than plenty noted political biographies.

The first time he and I met was in The Top House pub across the road from Station House. Janet and I went there a couple of evenings most weeks and engaged in company while seated on high stools at the bar. Frank invariably sat alone at a table by the open fireplace keeping his own counsel for the most part and never presuming to impose upon the company of others. He was, I learned later, a respected district councillor and occasionally he would be joined by someone seeking advice or to complain about something going on in the community.

My own initial limited contact with Frank was when he came to the bar for another drink. Always polite and friendly he would order and while waiting he would engage with us asking Janet and myself how we were doing, what we were doing etc... never staying longer than it took to be served.

I was surprised, therefore, when he invited us to join him at a table one evening. He introduced himself, politely doffing his cap to Janet, and enquired about our backgrounds and life stories. In return he explained that he was a member of Coundon Labour Party and that having overheard some our conversations with the pub landlord and other drinkers, he had become intrigued by what he termed my *"obvious left of centre leanings."* The way he spoke was captivating. Frank had a gentle conversational style, quietly spoken, always stopping to listen when appropriate and never pressing a point. I could tell that Janet wasn't particularly interested in our political discourse, light as it was, but I found myself more engaged as the evening wore on. I sensed what was coming and was proved right a couple of weeks later when Frank invited me to a Labour Party meeting.

In my trade union mind I imagined a well ordered room replete with top table for officials and theatre style seating for lay members. What I got was the confined, smoke-filled committee room of Coundon Workingmens Club with its huge, dark wood, rectangular table around which was seated a small group of people shuffling papers and arranging agendas and reports.

My first impression of many already seated made me smile as most looked as if they had been let out of a nursing home for the evening. Frank introduced me to former councillor Joe Gordon and incumbent councillor Vic Archer, both in their eighties, Dora Tulip not far from her ninetieth birthday, Paul Worsnop, fortyish and who was then Wear Valley District Council's energetic and thoughtful Planning Officer. Next to Paul was Michael Burns, a bright and articulate trade union officer with the Transport & General Workers Union, local residents Gwen and Charles Kay, both retired yet spritely and vocal, councillor June Lee and Citizen's Advice volunteer, Bob Dawson, both committed members beyond their youth. I don't have a problem with age, not then nor now, but the scene which met me at that first meeting was not what I had imagined before attending what I thought would be a vibrant group of local people flying the flag for Labour.

To be fair I was made to feel extremely welcome and was referred to throughout the meeting by many as 'pet', 'honey' or 'son'. June Lee was particularly friendly and we went on to develop a relationship which, within a couple of years, would see us working together as councillor colleagues on

Wear Valley District Council. I made an initial impression giving a rundown of my trade union background and activities and then I sat and listened to interminable council housing reports, planning committee considerations and the state of the street lights, footpaths and verges.

Nothing overtly political was discussed. Remember, this was a time when the troubles in Ireland still made the news, interest rates had risen to fifteen percent and Margaret Thatcher was standing firm against striking miners. The nearest we got to discussing anything political was a depressing autopsy of Bob Dawson's recent defeat in a council bye-election.

"I wasn't impressed, Frank," I said when I drove him home after the meeting.

"Oh," he said with surprise. "Whatever was the matter?"

I told him I'd expected to hear at least some political discussion about national and international affairs. I also said that the discussion they'd had on Bob Dawson's election defeat focussed mainly on who hadn't done enough, who had failed to do this, that and whatever, and that the lack of cogent analysis of the defeat had left me somewhat bemused.

"You'll find that's how our meeting are," said Frank.

"Well, I won't be joining", I retorted.

As a matter of fact, I did join. Janet did too. Frank proved gently yet powerfully persuasive saying that my naivety needed tempering because housing, highways and other local concerns were as much a part of national politics as anything debated in Westminster. I offered my view that whenever a general election was called, there didn't appear to be much evidence of physical activity being given to the campaign by the current Coundon Party membership.

"What do you do to attract others? Particularly younger people?" I asked.

"I don't know about the others," he replied, "but *I* do it by doing what I did with you when we first met."

"But isn't there any specific campaign to attract new members?"

"No. It takes money and people, neither of which we have in Coundon at the moment."

The fact that within twelve months I had been elected chairman of the branch says more about the moribund state of Coundon Labour Party at the time than any particular ability of mine. During the year since I had joined we had gained a handful of new members; Charlie Kay, the son of Charles and Gwen, along with his girlfriend Fiona, both in their twenties and engaged to be married. Jim Kean, a garrulous Scotsman originally from Gatehouse Of Fleet, and his wife Maisie who both brought views and opinions to the meetings. Jim had designs on becoming a councillor himself. In addition we drew in Gordon Henderson, a highly vocal albeit parochial campaigner for improvements in his home village of Binchester and, Gordon Hepple who worked on maintenance projects for Sedgefield District Council and Paul Hughes, a local government official with Easington District Council. In addition I was particularly delighted to draw in Lillian Denham. Lillian, or Lilly, saw no obstacles, said things as she saw things, took no prisoners, cajoled and encouraged the shy or unwilling and generally got stuck in. Tireless she was. She and Janet were polar opposites but became firm friends.

Lilly lived alone, frugal, in a sparsely furnished, two room thatched cottage next to the war memorial in Coundon and was always ready and available for campaigning and delivering leaflets. We have mourned the passing of many of those we knew back then but of them all, Janet was most affected when she found Lilly in bed, dead, alone. Such sadness still pervades.

In February 1985 I was appointed to be one of the branch delegates to Bishop Auckland Constituency Labour Party (CLP). The role was an important political development for me providing a bi-monthly insider view of Party operations and how these fed into national politics via the regional office, Labour North in Newcastle. In addition I was now receiving Parliamentary reports from our Member of Parliament, Derek Foster, now deceased but who went on to attain the title of Lord Foster of Auckland. Charlie Kay and I were also sent to fill vacant governor positions at both Close House and Eldon Lane Primary schools.

111

My first taste of the intense rivalry which often arises in local politics came during my first meeting of the governors' at Eldon Lane Primary School. Billy Neilson, Derek Foster's election agent, seasoned Labour Party campaigner and chair of the council's Housing Committee, asked to meet Charlie and myself in the schoolyard ten minutes prior to the start of the meeting. I had seen pictures of Billy in local newspapers, always besuited with his shock of wavy, nicotine stained hair and silver rimmed glasses which turned dark in bright sunlight. I was also aware of his extensive local knowledge so deftly deployed in dealings with the press on behalf of Derek Foster. His public persona and no-nonsense reputation meant I was rather looking forward to meeting him.

Billy wanted to "warn" us about a fellow governor we had yet to meet, the Liberal Democrat councillor, Chris Foote-Wood who, according to Billy, was *"a cunt."* We were told that he and Chris would be standing for election to the Chair of Governors and our votes would be crucial for Billy. The eventual vote went to a stalemate with both men receiving four votes each. That it took the best part of an angry and heated hour to agree how to resolve the impasse only confirmed what I'd heard about the intensity of their personal rivalries.

In the end, depleted of all argument and counter-argument and steered by the county council's most patient and diplomatic of officers, Doug Hutchinson and the school's embarrassed headteacher, Mr.Percival, the non-political governors, sat ashen faced and silent as the decision was reached by the drawing of lots. Chris Foote Wood was duly elected.

Notwithstanding the respect I gave to Billy's wealth of political experience, I prefer to make up my own mind about people. There was no doubting, however, the almost constant vitriolic scorn meted out by both these Labour and Lib-Dem luminaries, and I saw over the course of many years that Chris Foote Wood could indeed be, yes, *"a cunt"* from time to time and devious and cunning all of the time.

And yet our own political and personal relationships never strayed onto the wrong side of personal ill feeling. In fact, I came to the view that Chris positively enjoyed being a thorn in Labour's side. He certainly seemed to relish the cut and thrust of raucous debate in the theatre which was the council chamber and he revelled in the inevitable attention of the press... even when he was the subject of negative publicity. Chris was driven by personal ambition and the dream of attaining power. Throughout the many years I have known him I can't recall an election in which he didn't stand and fail to win; district council, county council, European Parliament and even Westminster Parliament. He never gave up, though, and in 2017 he lost again in the election for Mayor of Teesside only to then leave the Lib-Dems and apply to join the Labour Party. That his application was accepted came as a surprise to many, myself included.

My role as a school governor spanned twenty one years and I can see now why a handful of managers at Royal Mail became exasperated at my many requests for special leave. For in addition to Eldon Lane Primary and Close House Primary schools, I was later similarly appointed to Coundon Primary, Coundon St. Joseph's Primary, King James I Secondary and Bishop Auckland College. In due course governorships were reduced by statute to just two schools and my workload and special leave requests were significantly reduced to Coundon Primary and Close House Primary. For the majority of those twenty one years I was chairman of the governors at both.

I look back and wonder how on earth I managed. What with my roles in the Labour Party, the Trade Union, NHS Trust Boards and as a councillor, my work, lifestyle and home issues required a deal of careful planning and consideration. I was helped in the main by the love and support of my wife Janet who would later become a school governor herself and, in 1995, a district councillor. There would have been no chance in hell that I could have carried out such a range of demanding community representations without her support and understanding.

When I had met Chris Foote Wood at that first meeting of the governors, he was the leader of the Lib-Dem group on

Wear Valley District Council and a man whose ability to rile the calmest of Labour councillors was renowned. I know enough of the general nature of the majority of Lib-Dems at local level to see that, all too often, they are nothing more than opportunists who sway with the breeze. By this I mean they first establish which way public opinion is going and then adopt a position in support irrespective of whether they fundamentally agree with the issue or not. Anyone in opposition can do that, of course. After all, the responsibility of running the council is in someone else's hands. As long as the Lib-Dem stance is in opposition to Labour and gives the electors a sense that one is being sincere and on their side, that is all that matters to them.

That was my view then and it remains so today. However, where Chris Foote Wood scores higher than some is that he is unarguably intelligent, articulate and knows how to use the press to his advantage. When I later became a district councillor I saw the manner in which he led his small political group expecting only their compliant loyalty and votes. Billy Neilson and the Labour group leader, John Richardson, himself a veteran powerhouse of many years service, gave Chris no quarter in the council chamber and Chris gave none in return. In the years which followed I too often fell into bouts of argumentative rivalry with Chris. There really was no other option. To ignore and not refute

Chris's unremitting verbosity and campaigning was to invite electoral defeat.

Whenever I needed to steal a march on Chris I brought into play an effective rebuttal strategy headed at first by Frank Webster and Michael Burns and, in later years, contesting County Council seats, by my election agent and family friend, Neil Stonehouse. It was tough going. The Northern Echo's Bishop Auckland reporter in the latter years of the nineteen eighties was Cliff Edwards, a man who I felt was surreptitiously anti-Labour and his reporting generally did not favour us. Cliff, I have no doubt, would professionally deny it adding that he merely reported the facts as they appeared to him. Of course! And yet, in spite of many bruising campaigns, I'm sure Chris Foote Wood will acknowledge that although our rivalry was at times tempestuous, we never slogged it out to the degree that he, Billy Neilson and John Richardson did across the council chamber.

By the middle of summer 1985 my new found activities within the Labour Party and my established trade union work were keeping me busy. At the time such commitments weren't particularly onerous. Janet and I had settled into our new home, we had no children and I had no designs nor desire to take on any further responsibilities. Indeed I had become more active as the chairman of Coundon Labour Party and my growing presence within the CLP had led to me being nominated to the Durham County and European Labour Parties. NHS Trust Boards and Parliamentary aspirations were still a few years away. So with the addition of my trade union workload, I felt that enough was enough.

In just two short years I had augmented my position within the Union of Communication Workers by being elected to the dual posts of Branch Secretary and Political Officer and was steadily advancing within the Labour Party at both branch and CLP level. And then, on June 21st 1986, our first son, Daniel, was born. Janet and I now had a family which brought about a whole raft of new responsibilities and we couldn't have been happier. The year also marked the point at which I consciously put away my guitar and took on no further performing engagements. Photography, too, was relegated to close friend commissions and family holidays. With parenthood my life choices changed.

The political wards in which Janet and I lived in 1986 consisted of the communities of Coundon, Leeholme, Westerton, Leasingthorne, Binchester and Newfield. And in neighbouring Coundon Grange ward there was Close House, Gurney Valley, Auckland Park, Eldon Lane, Bridge Place, Coronation and Rosemount. Such a vast, semi rural populous, in excess of five thousand people, required five councillors; three in Coundon and two in Coundon Grange. Historically, these five Wear Valley District Council seats had always been contested by Labour, the Lib-Dems and the Conservatives. Occasionally a well intentioned, single issue, Independent candidate fancied their chances for one of the seats. In 1986 Labour held sway with twenty six of the forty council seats.

Bob Dawson announced that he did not wish to stand in the next round of council elections due the following year on 7th May. He had tried valiantly to win a seat for Labour in a recent bye election but had been somewhat bruised by defeat. So, with current incumbents Vic Archer and Frank Webster wishing to retire, the Party in Coundon met to appoint its candidates and select a team for the contest. Those duly nominated following shortlisting and selection meetings were June Lee, Charlie Kay and yes... me.

Before I agreed to be nominated I felt it prudent to first check with my employer in case there were any implications or clashes of interest should I be subsequently elected. I made an appointment to meet the head of Personnel in Middlesbrough Mail Centre, a most helpful man whose name I do not recall. I was delighted to be told, *"We'd be failing in our duty as an employer if we did not encourage our employees to take up active roles within the community!"*

The Head Postmaster's Manual sets out the scope for special leave which may be taken for a variety of community roles. I make this point here because, whilst Royal Mail in its

118

status as a public sector employer (as it was then) was supportive of my aspirations, there was many a time over the subsequent twenty one years when a number of managers found it difficult to fully accept what I was doing. By that I don't mean that there was a problem with them accepting my actual status as a councillor, but a few found my special leave applications irksome on the grounds that, as I overheard one day, they thought perhaps I was "getting away with something". Bless them.

As far as I remember, though, none of my special leave applications were ever declined; challenged and questioned occasionally, yes. But never declined. There was a time or two, however, when the special leave I was requesting was shuttled upstairs for the 'attention' of the area manager. But such silly disruptive moves came to nought as long as I stayed within nationally agreed entitlements.

Things settled down somewhat in later years when Processing Manager, Kevin Harland told me the main problem he and his line managers had was that they often had no idea where I was from one week to the next. I could see what he meant and I agreed to submit what became known as a whereabouts sheet every week detailing where and when I would be 'out of office' and when I would be at work. In addition Kevin and I reached an agreement where my working hours would be 12:30pm till 8:30pm Monday to Friday but I would take paid leave till 5:30pm to carry out

119

my role as Branch Secretary (utilising this time to also attend to my political pursuits). From 5:30pm I did outward sorting in the mail centre with any special leave requests for evening commitments being considered.

Thursday May 7th 1987 brought an end to a month or so of highly organised election campaigning. June, Charlie, myself and the campaign team had attended public meetings, chatted to people on their doorsteps and in their homes and on the streets and I was delighted when we were all subsequently elected. "Wow", I thought. "First time, first win". I was happy too that my friend Bill Oxbrough had been elected unopposed to represent the nearby Escomb ward. Bill, Charlie and myself, being the new kids on the block in council, underwent induction and training sessions together and quickly found that amongst the older more experienced Labour councillors, we were known variously as a wet behind the ears novelty or a pain in the arse.

There had been a dampener to our election night celebrations, though. We had failed to get our two Labour colleagues elected in Coundon Grange where my nemesis, Chris Foote Wood and his Lib-Dem running mate, the likeable Geoff Harrison, took the seats there. Nevertheless, unable to contain my vain exuberance I threw both arms in the air at the news of my personal result, shouted out something immature like, "get in!" or some such and reopened a cut on my top lip which I'd sustained shaving before leaving for the count. The bleeding wouldn't stop and in spite of valiant efforts to stem the flow, my pristine white shirt was ruined with the blood. In a post-count press interview, journalist Cliff Edwards respectfully didn't make reference to this most noticeable of minor injuries. Nor did he personally congratulate me save for what words he required for his story.

Before a councillor may assume the duties required of the post a declaration and oath of office have to be sworn and signed in the presence of the council's chief executive officer. I took the oath and duly signed on the dotted line on Monday 11th May. I was now an officially elected district councillor with a hell of a lot to learn.

With each new four year term councillors are allocated a number of committee's to serve on; Planning, Environment, Economic Development, Leisure, Housing being the main ones. I was placed on the Planning and Environment committees along with a number of sub committee's and a range of outside bodies, village halls and the like. As an indication of my naivety, I did not know that councillors received a monthly allowance; a sum fixed by statute and appended to travel and subsistence payments.

"Have you got your form, bonny lad?" asked councillor Belle Bousefield after my first council meeting.

121

"Form? What form?" I replied.

"Your expenses form. I'll take it down to the Treasurer's for you."

Sensing my puzzlement, Belle showed me where the expenses forms were kept and went through the steps of filling one out of for me. I was non-plussed. I honestly thought the role of a councillor was entirely voluntary and I had no idea that allowances were paid. I never asked and nobody had told me. At least I can't be accused of going into politics for the money.

My role as a councillor kept me busy with all manner of public and social engagements and I was delighted and proud to take my seat in the council chamber. At first Charlie, Bill and I were often at odds with some of our fellow Labour councillors, some of whom patronised our youth and exuberance. We were the antithesis of most in the chamber with some notable exceptions in the Labour group where many were stuck in their ways and kow-towed to our Leader, John Richardson. Don't get me wrong. I liked them all and made friends with a fair few.

I particularly admired John Richardson, or JR as he was known. Here was a man of vast experience commanding a loyal, if too readily acquiescent Labour group. That doesn't mean I agreed with all that he said or did. But even then, such was his unambiguous forcefulness, he could dismiss any counter proposal or argument I might put to him with a withering look and a patronising choice of words often beginning with, *"now look, bonny lad..."* Lest I be accused of ageism I don't buy into the idea of age being the inevitable equivalent of wisdom. It ought to. But typically many of those with experience I have known throughout all walks of life have proved less wise than their contemporaries. Where age does bring wisdom, it is to be acknowledged, celebrated even. But where age brings intolerance, cynicism, pomposity and downright rudeness it should be exposed for the sham it is.

A small coterie of re-elected women councillors let it be known from the outset that they were the ones with experience. I could hear the assuredness in their conversations – little of it relating to politics, policy or strategic governance - and I could see it in their body language. The truth is the only experience the majority of these women possessed was that of a greater number of years in office. Their political pronouncements were often naive and left me cold, sometimes incredulous.

There was one occasion when a couple of them suggested to Charlie and myself that the Labour Member of Parliament for Derby North, Dennis Skinner, The Beast Of Bolsover, was actually a tory plant with a remit to disrupt the Parliamentary Labour Party. Perhaps I'm being too unkind? A number of my newfound male colleagues were just as bad. Nonetheless, we all got on reasonably well and worked effectively to ensure the dominance of our political group decisions - always with Chris Foote-Wood and his Lib-Dems taking every opportunity to make life difficult for us.

There were a number of induction and training courses to attend in those early days and Charlie, Bill and I were shipped off to Aston University in Birmingham to be given a grounding in the complexities of local government finance. I can't say the course was particularly interesting, in fact we were bored most of the time. Nevertheless, being given millions of pounds of 'pretend' public money to spend on council services while maintaining strict budgets, meant that we came home with certificates showing we were more than capable of bankrupting Wear Valley District Council.

I particularly enjoyed meeting the electorate in groups and as individuals. Such times would either be facilitated via a phone call seeking my assistance or to complain about some issue or other. Other times would be through my attending the various community groups and outside bodies to which I had been appointed. I was particularly proud to lay a wreath on behalf of the council on Remembrance Sunday each year.

My allocated cenotaph was in Newfield where I had often attended with my predecessor, Frank Webster. When Frank retired I assumed the role and he would come to watch me lay the wreath. Janet always attended and, after our sons Daniel and Padraic were grown a little, they did too. The nice thing about Newfield was that there was always a good turnout of people paying respect to those who had died as a result of conflict. In a lot of communities councillors often cut a lone figure laying their wreaths.

The service of remembrance commenced in the village chapel where I would join in with the hymns and listen to words spoken with reverence and solemnity by the warm and welcoming Methodist minister, Willie Willis. I was not then of any religious persuasion. I remain not so today. As an aside, though, I respect all religions. However, what I do not respect are some of those who practise theirs.

My first wreath laying ceremony is one I shall never forget. I had been looking forward to the occasion and had kept in mind what I had seen Frank do so many times before – walk to the iron railings, open the gate and enter, lay the wreath on the step of the cenotaph, take two steps back, bow, turn and leave to rejoin the throng. What could possibly go wrong?

Singing over, our sizeable entourage made its way from the chapel and out to the village green and the cenotaph. More prayers and a hymn led to the appointed hour and a minute or so before 11am, wreath in hand, I made my way forward.

Now, the cenotaph in Newfield, prior to being relocated some years later, was situated on an upwardly rising slope necessitating that the gate be opened outwards. What did I do? Yes. I pushed it inwards. I pushed and pushed and the bottom of the metal gate became firmly stuck on the inclined concrete path leading to the towering obelisk. Conscious of dozens of eyes upon my back I tried to pretend that all was well and squeezed my way through the narrow gap. The result was that two buttons of my overcoat got caught on the gate frame and were torn off with such force they audibly whizzed through the air above the heads of the solemn celebrants. Those who could do so remained stoically silent as I carried on with the rest of the process with what little dignity I had left. I heard muffled chuckles from others.

I enjoyed being a councillor and was supportive of my ward, its people and their families and communities. I feel I represented their concerns openly and diligently and was, by and large, well respected. Actually, it might best be put this way... out of those three thousand or so electors, more than seventy percent of whom never bother to vote, I reckon that thirty or forty individuals saw me as a most hard working and diligent councillor with a similar number seeing me as a complete waste of space and not to be trusted. Then there was the remainder, that vast majority who just don't see their lives, environment, jobs, taxes, social care, education, laws and everything else as being the product of politics and political decisions.

I was an unyielding supporter of initiatives designed to bring investment, jobs and sustainability to the wider council area, too. With housing, planning and environment issues I played my part and I believe I contributed well in debates. Council officers would present reports for consideration and, when voted upon, would either be rejected or became council policy for implementation.

I judged one particular officer, Les Morgan, as bright, articulate and far sighted. He headed up the Leisure department and his brief included responsibility for public spaces, recreation grounds and swimming pools. Les's department also had managerial responsibility for Leisure Centres and, in particular, Spectrum Leisure Centre in Willington with its popular indoor dry-run ski slope. It was from this dry ski standpoint that Les drew up a scheme for discussion designed to bring tourism, revenue and jobs to the towns and villages in Weardale. He saw potential in the undulating landscape of the dale, with the river Wear flowing through it, to accommodate three or four dry-ski slopes on the southern hillsides rolling down to a holiday village hosting a range of activities – canoeing, horse riding, archery, fishing, cycling – plus chalets, shops and a hotel. Dozens of jobs, albeit the majority being part time, would be created and the resultant revenue would ameliorate the dale following the decimation of once traditional, mainly mining, industries.

Alas, in spite of the overwhelming support of the Labour group, our Lib-Dem councillors picked up on an element of public cynicism. Dales people had long harboured a degree of anger at the loss of local jobs and a minority expressed the view that reinvestment in manufacturing and mining would be preferable to tourism. They had a point, of course. Unfortunately, as much as the council would have jumped for joy at such investment, we were and still are in times where such is simply not forthcoming. Nevertheless, the ever iconoclastic Lib-Dems, backed by a rump of Weardale Independent councillors began to pour scorn on the plans whipping up increasing public opposition as the debate rumbled on.

Incredibly, The Northern Echo came out in cynical opposition also. Les Morgan and the council were subject to almost constant public and press derision and ridicule from then on. I couldn't understand it. Was I being naive? Here was a vision designed not just to introduce prosperity but to bring the dale into the twentieth century. A vision which was being scorned by the very people whose lives and livelihoods would benefit from its success. I created a bit of a stir during a heated council debate when, in support of the plans and imploring folk to see the financial and community advantages of its realisation, I publicly declared the objectors within the chamber and the people of Wear Valley 'culturally inept'.

The seeds of the demise of Labour's power in the council had now been sown. Of all the negative issues which are

128

inevitably levelled at controlling council groups ahead of an election, the ski village was the key driver to Labour being ousted from power in 1991 and the Lib-Dems assuming control. Les Morgan had had enough and moved away to Scotland, John Richardson survived an election night heart attack and I, along with swathes of others lost my seat.

6 – Any Port In A Storm

I'd had a productive and enlightening four year tenure as a district councillor and, as a keen advocate for democracy, I accepted that the people had spoken. Moreover, I understood that the result had been an 'anti-Labour council' vote and was nothing personal against myself. I remained active within the Labour Party continuing my various roles as I had always done and, as far as the union was concerned, nothing changed there either. The only difference was that I was no longer a councillor and could spend more time with Janet and our two sons, Daniel, now nearly five and Padraic who was born in October the previous year.

Further developments were afoot, however, and following a meeting of The European Constituency Labour Party in Spennymoor Recreation Centre I was approached by one Walter Nunn. Walter, then in his eighties, lived in Shildon, had been a councillor for most of his adult life and was a socialist who steadfastly remained wedded to principle and honour. A staunch advocate for people, he fought against all manner of injustice without fear or favour. A burning hatred of the tories ran in his blood.

Walter is perhaps best remembered for his finest hour, although sadly one which eventually beat him, in leading the campaign to save Shildon's railway workshops when they were faced with closure. The shops, as they were known locally, were world famous and were *the* major employer in the town. Campaigning relentlessly Walter, along with our Member of Parliament Derek Foster, local councillors and trade unionists, took the fight all the way to the European Parliament, never ceasing nor tiring until defeated when the shops closed in 1984.

As I made my way through the recreation centre car park following the European Committee meeting Walter wound down his car window and invited me in to his passenger seat. We shook hands and I asked him what he wanted.

"I'll tell you what I'm after, Phil and I'll get straight to the point."

"Go on," I said.

"We need someone young like you to stand for CLP Secretary."

"What?" I exclaimed. "Me!?"

"Yes! You."

He shuffled round in his seat and turned to face me.

"The annual meeting is next March," he said. "You've got plenty of time to prepare yourself and I'll make sure there's enough of a turn-out to vote you in if there's any opposition."

"But what about Bob Fleming?" I enquired of the current secretary.

"Don't worry about him," he offered. "Everything will be alright."

132

I told him I was highly flattered but I couldn't see how I could possibly take on any more responsibilities with everything else that I had going on. He didn't flinch and I sensed that he couldn't care less about my protestation. He repeated that I was the one for the job and that I'd be letting down both the CLP and himself if I didn't go for it.

"Give Bob Fleming a call", he advised, "and get yourself around to his house sometime so he can show you the ropes."

Before I knew it I was saying 'okay' and thanking him for the approach. It wasn't until during the drive home that I asked myself what the hell I was letting myself in for.

Bob Fleming and his wife Angie were most helpful and happy to have me in their home one evening where, over cups of coffee, I was given an insight into the role of the CLP Secretary. Bob produced mountains of files and paperwork consisting mainly of minutes of meetings, reports, membership lists and correspondence. I saw that a lot of it was handwritten and I wondered how he managed to get everything written down and distributed to the sixty or so delegates every two months on top of dealing with all the correspondence, phone calls and general enquiries. He then reminded me that there was an executive committee of the CLP which met every alternate month which I'd need to attend too.

At least Bob's filing system seemed perfectly organised although a lot of it was contained in copious carrier bags. I was shown an electronic typewriter, a recent purchase by the CLP. At least that's something, I thought. Bob told me he also had access to a photocopier which was kept in Bishop Auckland at the home of Party member, Norman Button. Until Helen Goodman became the Member of Parliament in 2005, CLP secretaries in Bishop Auckland ran things from their homes and were presented with a bottle of sherry and a pack of mint chocolates from the House of Commons shop at Christmas time. Derek Foster employed his wife Ann in Westminster and Billy Neilson worked for him from a small, single desk, rented office in Shildon. Helen put an end to this unsatisfactory state of affairs when she opened a constituency office in Bishop Auckland and staffed it appropriately.

Angie Fleming assured me that things looked worse than they actually were when spread across their dining table and that, with a bit of organisation, I'd be fine doing the job. And, over time, so it proved. The following March I was elected unopposed and took my seat at CLP meetings next to our treasurer John Dormer, President Michael Burns and our Member of Parliament, Derek Foster. It was a position I would hold for the next ten years during which time I dragged the administration into the modern world by getting the CLP to purchase a computer.

To carry out the role effectively it was necessary to work closely with fellow CLP officers. The sharing of information and timely notices is paramount to avoiding problems and keeping schedules, especially during those years before the internet, email and mobile technology. My closest ally was the then Membership Secretary, Marjorie Kellett. She and I became friends and I depended upon her calm and steady methodology to keep me on track.

I never once saw Marjorie angry or ruffled. I'm sure she had her moments but, in the main, she remained stoic in the face of troubling issues preferring, as she did most humorously on occasion, to take the pee out of situations and people. I admit to sharing that trait with her. Marjorie's sense of fun and our working friendship kept our chins up whenever the going got tough. The only time it was not wise to telephone Marjorie was during her coveted daily listening to The Archers on BBC Radio 4. I learned that very early in our relationship.

There was a storm brewing however. The Labour Party was rolling out its policy of all women shortlists in an effort to ensure gender equality across all positions from constituencies through to seats in Parliament. Support for and opposition to the policy raged in arguments throughout the country and as secretary of Bishop Auckland CLP I was charged by delegates to inform Labour North, the Party's regional office in North Shields, that we would not accept the policy under any circumstances.

The matter had been discussed in a noisy meeting in a hired room in King James 1 Secondary School where our women members rose, too, to speak against the idea. Walter Nunn almost exploded in his condemnation and Bob & Angie Fleming roused others to declare, 'all women shortlists will not be accepted in Bishop Auckland'. The overwhelming justification, from women in particular, was that if a man was ideally suited then it would be madness to offer the role to a woman who was not as ideally suited simply because of dictat. The point was also made that a woman more ideally suited than a man should likewise be given the post. And then a number of women stated that the idea would be an affront to their dignity if they were perceived to have gained a position through gender as opposed to ability. We were blessed with some outstandingly talented women in the CLP and they, in turn, recognised their outstandingly talented male colleagues. What was needed, they felt, were better ways to enable women to step forward in their own right through opportunity, training and support. Our MP, Derek Foster, wisely and rightly stayed clear of the issue.

Thus instructed to inform our regional director, Eric Wilson, I wrote a detailed letter outlining Bishop Auckland CLP's opposition to all women shortlists and carefully composed the reasons why we would not comply. I could hear the drums of war beating as I dropped the envelope in the post box. Sadly for me the anticipated brouhaha resulted not with me being caned by regional office but by my colleagues in the CLP. The reply instructing me to inform delegates that compliance was expected arrived within days and I filed it aside to report to the following week's executive committee.

When I presented the letter to the committee their response was rather more measured and muted than previously. Measured and muted, perhaps, but equally adamant that because the CLP had agreed unanimously not to accept all women shortlists, I had better write again to reaffirm our position.

My second letter raised the stakes somewhat and I was summoned to the regional office. War drums were indeed beating but the mood was amicable as I reiterated that which I had been instructed to say. In return I was told to convene a meeting and inform delegates, backed up by a letter from Labour North, that unless compliance was met there would be an inquiry which could result in CLP officers being removed and the running of the constituency placed in the hands of the regional executive. Strong stuff. In fact, no inquiry was necessary. Faced with what amounted to sequestration I was left with no option but to inform delegates that continuing with the policy of non-compliance

137

would be tantamount to the disestablishment of our roles in the CLP and that, subsequently, all women shortlists would be introduced regardless. As it seemed to me, we could not win this argument.

And that's what I reported back to the CLP. I gave a clear assessment of the situation and reasoned that to avoid a damaging confrontation, we should accept the policy but remain vigilant when the time came for selections. I suggested to members that we could still seek to retain an element of control over whoever was eventually selected. After all Bishop Auckland hadn't yet been officially declared an all women shortlist constituency. I wasn't instructing – merely advising. And that's when I was subjected to the most vitriolic onslaught of my political life as one by one, delegate after delegate rose to accuse me of selling the CLP down the river, of capitulating too readily, of being in cahoots with regional office and... of lying.

None of what I was being accused was remotely true. I gave a lengthy and detailed response outlining my own position and involvement adding that, as with the delegates, I opposed the idea of all women shortlists. However, I urged that emotion be excluded from the debate and to consider the obvious and unstoppable disruption that would beset the CLP if we continued. One by one, slowly but surely, the majority of delegates gave way, albeit reluctantly, thereby avoiding the most inevitable of internal showdowns which the press would have reported with uncontrolled glee.

If my memory serves me well, regional office then offered a compromise of sorts which stated they would not actually impose all women shortlists on Bishop Auckland but would review their position as and when future selections were due. Helen Goodman was selected from an all woman shortlist in 2005...with, guess what?... no resistance whatsoever from delegates! Work that one out.

Time passed and the vitriol and bitterness which had been aimed in my direction dissipated sufficiently for the debacle to be left behind. I now devoted my energies to being a husband and father at the same time as fulfilling my other roles in the Labour Party and in the trade union. My part time photography business, FILMAR Photography, was well established by now and weddings and sports event were a feature of many weekends. P & E Photographics had folded following my move away from Tudhoe in 1982 and I had lost contact with my former business partner Ed Spence.

The new business name, FILMAR Photography, came from an association with a postman colleague in Darlington who, like me, enjoyed photography beyond mere snapshots. Martin Garraway and I set up the joint enterprise using part of our first names – Phil (FIL) and Martin (MAR). In due course, though, Martin left Royal Mail and moved away from the area leaving me to carry on with what was to become a lucrative and successful sole trader business.

But what was mainly exercising my mind in 1992 was the forthcoming Durham County Council elections. Chris Foote Wood held the Coundon seat for the Lib-Dems and I was selected to try and beat him and regain it for Labour. It would be no mean feat and I knew it would be a tough contest. The election was scheduled for the following May giving myself and my team almost a year to prepare. My accumulated experience of Chris Foote Wood and of how he operated gave me an edge when the contest started in earnest the following March.

Supported by the organising skills of Frank Webster and Michael Burns, heading up a hard working team of canvassers from within the branch, I drew on my earlier popularity as a district councillor and raised my presence throughout the ward by increasing my attendance at local events in schools, churches and community halls. My role as chair of governors at both Coundon and Close House Primary schools was a good starting point in maintaining relations with parents and grandparents, too. From a campaigning perspective there was a lot more ground to cover compared with the district council elections because the county council ward included both Coundon *and* Coundon Grange wards and totalling some five thousand or more people. I wasn't as well known in Coundon Grange so it was prudent to devote a lot of time there. The strategy worked. The feedback during canvassing was very positive and on Thursday 1st May 1993 I achieved what some thought might not be possible; I unseated Chris Foote Wood and was elected as a Durham County Councillor.

"By heaven, Phil", exclaimed Frank Webster after the count. "You've done it. You've beaten footy wood!"

News of my election was quickly relayed from the county council to the various public bodies and village halls and I was invited to meet many of those with whom I would be working and representing. As well as my fundamental role representing individual members of the public I saw these 'outside' bodies as mini-powerhouses where local initiatives and schemes were drawn up and put into practise on behalf of whole communities. The George Pitt Reclamation Scheme in Escomb was one such.

Chaired, steered and cajoled by the larger than life Reverend Nick Beddow and where England's smallest Saxon church is still used today for worship, this local group worked as a critical friend to developers and in keeping watch on matters pertaining to the village. And so, on a pleasant sunny evening two or three weeks after the election, I found myself in the splendid confines of the living room in the vicarage with Nick and the Lib-Dem district councillor for the area, Vince Perkins, along with a couple of residents.

We were discussing matters of interest when during a comfort break Nick took me aside.

"When I say *'any port in a storm'* indicate that you need to be moving on."

The meeting resumed and after half an hour or so had passed, I got the intriguing signal. Making a point of looking at my watch and feigning surprise, I played along with Nick's instruction.

"I really need to press on, ladies and gentlemen. It's been wonderful meeting you all and I look forward to our working together."

At that the others fired back their various farewell's, picked up pens and papers, coats and hats and began to leave. Nick let his guests out into the late spring evening air and ensured we were alone.

"Come with me", he said. "Sit back down and let's have a proper chat."

I did as he suggested and was served a glass of vintage port. Ha, ha. Nice joke. Nick took a high backed armchair opposite and slowly savoured a mouthful.

"Right!" he said quietly but with a hint of authority. "Now that you're elected we need to get on to get things done. Do you understand what I mean?"

"Erm. Not exactly, Nick, but please go on."

"It's like this. I need you on board with some ideas I have for the village and you need me because I know the electorate and the clergy where you operate."

Blackmail? Tenacity? Canny business? Call it what you will. I can only ponder, apart from my being vice chair of the county council's Environment Overview & Scrutiny Committee, what was stirring in the mind of my reverend acquaintance. Draw your own conclusions, too, as to why Vince Perkins wasn't sharing the port with us.

Nick and I became close friends and we would share NHS Trust Board status as non-executive directors within a few years. Sadly, he succumbed to Multiple Sclerosis which grew slowly and progressively worse. But before invalidity got too firm a hold on his body, he gained a degree of public notoriety for smoking cannabis attesting to its medicinal qualities and palliative uses. He risked being arrested. Nonetheless, in order to press home the message about the narcotic benefits, he appeared on television news announcing his intention to travel to Holland, where cannabis was legally available in a number of outlets, and be filmed smoking the stuff. He did, too. The media loved it.

The Vicar Who Went To Pot! ran one headline. Sadly, Nick died in January 1998 aged just 50. Bill Oxbrough, also a family friend of Nick's, drove he and I to the funeral and celebratory mass in the neighbouring village of Witton Park. There, among a host of others, we had standing room only outside the church such was the heaving mass of mourners. The village street was brought to a standstill. Newspaper columnist, Mike Amos, wrote in his Northern Echo column, ' ...*a life rich and refulgent, a ministry maverick, majestic and once or twice plain mad...*and...*a man of enthusiasm and of endless exuberance, of vision, a man of great kindness and sometimes of much cussedness, too.*' Fitting.

7 – Changing Times

By now my UK-wide network of colleagues and friends within the union had grown immeasurably. Of many there have been none closer than Mike Findley. Originally from Tooting, an ardent lifelong Fulham FC supporter, Mike moved to Redcar as a young postman in 1978. There he met his future wife, Judith, and they became proud parents to their lovely daughter, Rachel.

I first met Mike when he became a District Organiser in 1986. His voice, deep and sonorous, never lost its strong 'sarf' London accent and was well matched to his deep set, dark eyes, ala film actor Omar Sharif. In addition for many years he sported a heavy 'easy rider' moustache in the style of the actor Dennis Hopper. With an ability to laugh in the face of any difficulty, Mike proved to be a confident union official who always saw a glass half full as opposed to half empty.

"Oi never warry abaht anyfing which Oi 'ave now controwl owver", he would say.

It was a remarkably apt adage and one which in time would serve him with strength and dignity when in 2005, still in his prime of life, he was stricken with Motor Neurone Disease. The doctors gave him two years to live. He proved them wrong and overcame all manner of difficulties with the disease's insidious spread. Wheelchair bound, in need of care for all manner of life's necessities and, although physically weakened, he remained positive, focussed and, at times, pissed off. I found him utterly inspirational.

Mike didn't drive and relied on public transport and friends with cars to cover the vast north east region. With workplaces as far north as Newcastle Upon Tyne and to the south as far as Doncaster, I don't recall him ever being late for meetings, briefings or member representations. He maintained and managed his ever ready union presence from an office in Teesside Mail Centre and from his home in Marske By The Sea.

In tandem with his union positions - District Organiser until 1990, North East Regional Secretary till 1992 and Divisional Representative to 1998 - Mike was also a Labour councillor in Redcar, later to leave the Party and stand as an Independent. He kept his seat on the council until stepping down in 2018. When he was elected as Mayor of the borough in 2008, he became something of a local celebrity through relentless charity work raising huge sums for local causes. Prior to his mayoral activities he had launched the Mike Findley MND Fund with a "Morning Of Music" in Marske Square on Saturday 15th September 2005. The event was a huge success and now takes place every year. In addition to raising money for research into MND, and for which there is currently no cure, Mike also donated from his many charitable events to the MND Care Centre in James

Cook University Hospital in Middlesbrough, as well as giving donations to help local people suffering with the disease. In a fitting acknowledgement of his charitable greatness, in June 2010 Mike, Judith and Rachel, along with Rachel's fiancé, Dean, attended Buckingham Palace where Mike was presented with an MBE by Her Majesty The Queen.

Fast forward for a moment to 2014 and a spring day in James Cook University Hospital. Having been retired since 2008 (although, as I have said earlier, I prefer to use the term 'retread') I was in the throes of recovering from Guillain Barre Syndrome, an illness which left me paralysed from the neck down for the best part of ten months. News reached me that Mike had been brought in to hospital with a painful urinary infection. Janet wheeled me to his ward where, with him lying in bed and me in my wheelchair alongside, we discussed politics and the many people we knew within the trade union and Labour movements, laughing and joking at all manner of shared memories.

"Ya now wot, Phil?" he said. "MND may 'ave chynged my loife, baht... it wown't chynge *me*!"

Priceless.

In 1992 Mike stood down from the post of Regional Secretary to take one of two Divisional Representative posts, created following the introduction of the Industrial Relations Framework. His divisional counterpart, based in Sheffield, was Gary Hodkinson and the two worked together supporting trade union officers and branches in what was meant to be a new era of industrial relations. In essence there was now an unambiguous structure to follow to resolve issues in the workplace. The Industrial Relations Framework augmented the status of workplace representatives and their line managers who were now charged with reaching agreements at the first level. Where agreements could not be reached the issue was to be elevated to divisional level and, if an impasse occurred at that stage, the final arbiters would be national officers and the employer. Simple, eh? Not quite! Inevitably, whilst the IR Framework had been sensibly constructed, easy to follow and simple in its intent, relations between local management and union officials became more strained.

As it seemed to me, the strain was symptomatic of the distrust which had become ingrained in many workplaces leaving neither party capable of sticking to the spirit of the framework. This most helpful tome, as I said earlier, was ignored in the main by managers and used as a weapon by union officials.

The nineties represented a decade of change for myself and my growing family. Following the death in May 1994 of Labour's leader, John Smith, a man I very much admired and whom I had the privilege of meeting on a number of occasions, the Party drew together to mourn and then elect a successor. Enter Tony Blair who became leader of the Party on June 21st. Whatever one's views and opinions about Tony, and history is likely to judge him unfairly and unfavourably, he breathed new life into politics at the time.

The cruel ravages of the community destroying Thatcher governments were keenly felt across the country. Disposable income and living conditions had fallen, employment opportunities grew less, and society in general was fractured. Unless, that is, you happened to be part of the established tory supporting elite in which case you would have been well cushioned from the impact of such cruel and divisive right wing policies. Tony went on to lead the country as Prime Minister with far reaching, radical policies which brought an undeniable element of hope and rising prosperity to millions.

What can not be ignored is that Tony Blair, his government and policies were overwhelmingly popular enough to win three consecutive general elections; a feat never before achieved since the founding of the Party in 1906. Labour's policies from 1997, forward thinking and formulated through having learned the lessons of an oft-times disastrous history, and which brought about positive advancements in education, the NHS, the police and society as a whole, are now largely forgotten by todays Party members and have been cruelly and spitefully reversed by

149

the tories. In spite of his government's many successful and welcome domestic policies Tony's legacy is assured, incorrectly in my opinion, for the UK's role in middle east wars. Still, he was the right man for the time. But time moves on.

My own relationship with Tony goes back to the time before he became an MP and looking for a seat to contest. History tells us of his soon to be agent, John Burton along with Phil Wilson and Paul Trippet; this latter being the steward of what was then Trimdon Workingmans Club. These three men introduced Tony to the members of Sedgefield CLP who then went on to select him to be their candidate at the next general election. There's an interesting quiz question which crops up from time to time – "Who was the MP for Sedgefield before Tony Blair?" I'll let readers dwell on that question and for those who don't know, I'll give the answer in a little while.

For my part, though, I had met Tony at a number of political events and meetings and I became a vocal supporter of his 'third way' ideology seeing it as essential to the change which was so desperately needed throughout the country. His vision of a future where neither private enterprise nor public body held a monopoly on being right, resonated within and outside of the Party at the time. To some Party members though the idea of utilising the very best from either sector is anathema to socialist thinking. But then again, there are those who prefer the comfortable passion of protest in opposition as opposed to the power and responsibility of leading in government.

The Sedgefield and Bishop Auckland constituencies share adjacent borders. As a result their respective officers and a number of members are known to each other with some long established friendships having been forged. I had regular contact with Sedgefield CLP secretary, Rita Taylor. In addition, when Tony became a member of the shadow cabinet having been given the Trade & Industry brief, I had occasion to deal with him both in person and through John Burton on behalf of CWU members in postal industries. Subsequently he was acutely aware of my stated support for what he felt was needed to be done if and when Labour regained power.

During a warm summer evening in 1994, at an art exhibition in County Hall in Durham, Janet and I were in the midst of an invited audience of county councillor colleagues and their wives and husbands. The exhibition of Durham history themed glass panel displays by local artists was to be opened by none other than Tony Blair himself. He was universally popular at the time and his arrival at the event was much anticipated. Orange juice, white and red wine and canapés were served as we chatted and waited in the vast expanse of The Durham Room.

Now, being the pleb that I am, I had assumed that 'art exhibition' equated to an informal dress code and Janet and I attended in our jeans and casual tops. Whapwaaah!! Everyone else was in suits and dresses. Oh, the derisive looks we were given. Nevertheless, we weren't overly embarrassed and introductions and conversations flowed amicably enough. Then we heard the signal, "the leader is arriving" and the suits and dresses pushed to be first in line. It was a lengthy line and Janet and I, too slow to respond, were in a row behind with a small number of others who had also been slow to react.

Over the sea of heads in front of us we could see Tony and his wife Cherie enter and be greeted by Council Leader Don Robson who proceeded to introduce them like a football club captain introducing royalty to his line-up of FA Cup finalists. Suits were anxious for their wives to be introduced to Tony and progress was slow as we waited dutifully behind the main activity. And then Tony spotted Janet and myself. At that very moment, using his impressive height, he reached out an arm with open hand over the heads of those in front of us.

"Ah, Phil. Janet. Hello you two. How're you doing?" he beamed as we shook hands.

"Fine, Tony", I answered. "It's good to see you. Catch you later if you're still around."

"Might have to dash".

"No problem. Good luck to you".

And with that he was away down the flesh pressing line once more, with a fair few now looking down noses in our direction.

And the answer to the question, "Who was the MP for Sedgefield before Tony Blair?".... Nobody! The Sedgefield seat was newly established as a result of recent boundary changes and Tony was its first MP. So, now you know if you didn't already.

The Communication Workers Union was formed on 26th January 1995 through the merger of the Union of Communication Workers and the National Communications Union. Thus was born the communications trade union we know today. This mighty organisation, consisting of 110,000 postal members represents workers not just in Royal Mail, Post Office and British Telecom members but also telephone engineers and catering staff. A major recruitment campaign has been ongoing since the merger and the CWU today has members in related industries such as O2, Cable TV, Accenture HR Services, Orange, Virgin Media and a host of others in computing, clerical, mechanical, driving, retail, finance and manual sectors.

During 1995 more storm clouds were gathering in the postal sector and CWU members braced themselves for what was to become a significant dispute. In an industry where strikes had been relatively unheard of, the last major national dispute had been in 1972, workers in the changing postal industry were set for an almost constant round of local walkouts, workplace ballots, and national strikes as we lurched towards the new millennium.

Royal Mail had designs on a wide ranging agenda for change; ostensibly, as they would have the country believe, to improve service delivery in the face of unsubstantiated future competition following deregulation of European-wide postal services. The crunch came with proposals to scrap second deliveries and introduce a single daily delivery with postmen and women staying out on the streets for longer and being served with additional bags of mail as they made their rounds. As an adjunct to this paragraph, when I started out as a postman in 1974, taking out just three bags of mail on the first delivery, each weighing up to thirty five pounds, was rare and considered a 'heavy' day. By 1995, three, four or five bags had become the norm and the move to one single delivery would see this rise to six, seven and beyond depending on mail volumes. It was a recipe for injury, sick leave and future musculo-skeletal problems for postal workers.

We were balloted for national industrial action in 1996 in defence of the second delivery and returned a vote of 3-1 in favour. At the same time the union submitted a claim for a shorter working week. In the face of pernicious anti trade

154

union legislation, industrial action could only proceed following a stalling timetable of notifications and verifications to the employer. Ostensibly, this is merely to satisfy the legal ramifications established by the tory government and, sadly, continued under Labour. In essence, however, it was a political device to lessen the impact of industrial action by giving notice to the employer and thus, give time to prepare mitigation and conduct a public propaganda campaign against the forthcoming action. There are always two sides in a dispute but the tories had gleefully ensured that it was just the trade unions who were sequestrated.

Of the actual dispute, here's what my friend Mike Findley had to say as part of my research for this book...

In 1996 the postal workers voted 3 to 1 for an all-out strike in defence of the service (the second delivery) and in a claim for a shorter working week. This was converted into a series of one day strikes by the CWU leadership. The postal workers accepted this as they thought it would be just as effective in giving grief to the management. But the CWU leadership then issued so many exemptions from strike action that it was totally ineffective. The CWU (formed in 1995) was then headed by Alan Johnson who persuaded the union's National Executive Committee to call off the one day strikes without any of them having seen the agreement he

155

had supposedly signed with the management. When it was clear that there was no agreement the strikes resumed and despite lots of unofficial action the union leadership were still able to keep some control of the movement via one day strikes (without even telling some workers who was on strike and who was not). It was a recipe for demoralisation - exactly as the union leadership wanted. It ushered in a new period of macho management in the post office. Within a few months Johnson was elected as a Labour MP and despite (or perhaps because of) once declaring his allegiance to the Communist Party of Great Britain (i.e. the pro-Moscow Stalinists) soon became a Blairite minister in the new Labour Government after 1997.

The sense of demoralisation which Mike mentions was felt keenly throughout the country and especially in the twelve union branches which made up the CWU north east region. My own members throughout the Darlington branch area were increasingly critical of my own leadership and the part played by their workplace representatives.

I recall being at a meeting in Darlington with north eastern postal branch officers and representatives when a telephone call came through from the BBC to our chairman, Ken King. Journalists had learned that our collective concerns about the direction of the dispute was on our agenda for discussion and they wished to attend to film part of the proceedings and conduct an interview. Ken led our consideration of the request and we agreed to admit the film crew to shoot footage but not to record dialogue and that Mike Findley and guess who? yes, me, would be interviewed outside.

What went out on national television news a few hours later sent shockwaves through the union culminating in what we reckoned would have been a near explosion in CWU headquarters in London. Mike and I explained to the BBC that CWU members felt let down by our national leadership, that management in the workplaces had become increasingly belligerent having sensed our national disunity and that the sooner a cessation of the current hostilities could be brought about, the better. Members, we stated, needed a new agreement and that the current appetite for continuing with the strikes had dissipated. In effect, we concluded, "call off the strikes!"

What Mike and I had done, with the full support of the north east branches and by publicly stating the overwhelming views of our members, was risky. Of course we knew that. We knew we would bring public relations problems to the union's leadership in London.

Nevertheless, the views of our increasingly divided, frustrated and demoralised members mattered most to us. Surprisingly, not much was made of our 'indiscipline' except for a strident note by way of reminder, aimed at all union

157

officials, to 'go through headquarters on all such matters'. No blood spilled and no action was brought against either Mike or myself. Perhaps our leaders agreed with us?

It can be both satisfying and unnerving being in the public eye. Whenever my name appeared in a newspaper or my voice was heard on radio, people would say, "Hey, I see you were in the paper the other day" or, "I heard you on the radio this morning". I knew of course that my name and voice was what resonated and that the subject matter of which I was speaking was often given scant regard. And so it proved following my joint interview with Mike Findley. Calling in for a beer and to meet my brother on the way home later I was greeted at the bar in The Grey Horse pub in Shildon by two or three fellas telling me they had just seen me on the six o'clock news.

"Oh, really?" I said. "And what was I talking about?"

I received a collective, "I dunno! Some union stuff or other, wasn't it?" Enough said.

Mike's position as North East Region Divisional Officer came to a sudden and abrupt end in October 1998. He was defeated in that years election by Bob McGuire, Newcastle Amalgamated Branch Area Processing Representative. To some, myself included, the ballot result came as something of a surprise with Bob expected to do well but not at his first time standing for the post. Bob won convincingly, however, and the hurt felt by Mike, though carried with great dignity, was nevertheless palpable and he took early retirement in April 1999. Mike is remembered for his dedication and loyalty to union members and remained respected by many current and former CWU members and Royal Mail managers. Bob McGuire, in essence, has proved a most worthy successor and continues in his divisional role today. I count both men as friends.

8 – A Broken Promise

The country was in the grip of what was referred to as the 'beef crisis'. With news footage of burning pyres of Bovine Spongiform Encephalopathy (BSE) infected cattle carcases, an almost daily feature on tv news, radio and in newspapers, 1995 into 1996 was considered a nadir for anyone in politics or farming. Restrictions on the import and export of beef and countrywide cattle movements were slowly bringing sections of the agricultural industry to its knees. Public access to the countryside was severely curtailed and British beef was blacklisted around the world. Millions of pounds were spent dealing with the crisis and it took many months for the government and eminent scientists to arrive at a position where they could begin to quell public fears.

In time public confidence was regained and things returned to normal - helped via publicity stunt-crazy tory government minister, John Gummer MP, feeding a beefburger to his daughter on national television – and the beef industry slowly started to recover. Yet whilst there were scores of experts being rounded up to appear on radio, tv and in newspapers, each asserting that eating British beef was safe again, the decision whether or not to reintroduce it as a choice in school dinners was left to individual local authorities.

It fell to me, then, as vice chairman of the council's Environment Overview & Scrutiny Committee to lead the debate in County Durham. Committee members had copious reports from government and industry before them and council officers and a solicitor were on hand to provide procedural and legal advice. Our cross-party discussion was straightforward and we quickly moved to a unanimous vote being taken to reintroduce beef to school menu's where schools wished to do so. After a post-meeting recap with council officers to firm up the wording of a press release I left county hall to drive home for lunch and then take a walk with a new camera.

I had recently purchased a Nikon FE Single Lens Reflex camera with nine frames per second motordrive and I was anxious to put it through its paces. I needed to check all the settings and a walk in the countryside would provide the perfect conditions. Being built around a metal chassis, unlike today's modern SLR cameras with their plastic bodies, the FE was a hefty beast and difficult to hold steady with a large lens attached. To bear the weight I dug out a monopod to provide shooting steadiness and to carry the ensemble over one shoulder, shellelagh style.

With a fine summer afternoon to come I headed out down the former railway line from New Coundon towards Binchester. The sun shone and the sky was blue and cloudless. Birch, ash, hawthorn and beech were in leaf and birdsong filled the air and hedgerows. Peacefulness abounded and I stopped from time to time to capture on Ilford FP4 film some of the natural beauty which envelopes these south Durham parts.

An hour or so into the walk, having passed Binchester and turning west along the road C96 to Newfield I then headed south towards Bishop Auckland. My mobile phone rang.

"Hello. Phil Graham speaking."

"Ah, hello Councillor Graham. It's Nigel from the Press Office in County Hall. Are you free to talk?"

"I am but I'm out on a walk right now. What can I do for you?"

"We've had Tyne Tees television on. They're following up on the decision that was reached by your committee this morning."

"Yes. And?"

"They want to do an interview with you."

I explained that I was at least an hour away from home and suggested they might want to ask someone else. There was no one available apparently so I resolved to try to be home within the hour to conduct the interview from there...assuming Janet was available to come and collect me. Failing that, I'd ring back. I phoned Janet and explained the situation and she managed to leave work and drive out to meet me.

The television crew wanted to conduct the interview in one of the fields to the rear of my house. I had no objection because, fortuitously, there were cows in there. Curious cows, at that. We had to do around six takes as bovine inquisitiveness continually encroached upon the filming. Laughter and the odd freshly dropped cowpat were cut from the final edit and I'm pleased to say that the six o'clock news broadcast did not damage the council's or my personal integrity. Indeed the broadcast and the earlier press release brought more interview requests from local radio and newspapers.

With the exception of a handful of complaints, scorn and derision from vegetarians, one of whom declared the beef crisis an act of divine punishment upon human carnivores, I was once again thrust into the media spotlight for a week or two.

With regard to Labour's gradual re-emergence as a credible party of government I had always maintained in anecdote that John Smith had sowed the seeds, Neil Kinnock, most capable but constantly lampooned by large sections of the press, tended the crops and that Tony Blair reaped the harvest.

The sense of anticipation that Labour would win the forthcoming general election bore fruit on the morning of Friday May 2nd 1997. Exit polls from the night before had hinted at an overwhelming majority but it wasn't until the following early hours, with the new day awakening to bright spring sunshine, that I realised something truly momentous had dawned. The tories with their cruel, society wrecking policies had been ousted from office and Labour heralded in a new era of prosperity, opportunity and, above all, fairness and would be in government for the next thirteen years. I was absolutely thrilled.

To be fair you would be forgiven, looking back, for believing that the public mood was high only because of ejecting the tories. In fact there was more to it than that... Tony Blair was seen as the very antithesis of what the country had endured since 1979. Here was a promise of a new way forward with everyone included in a new, kinder, politics.

Phone calls started before breakfast. The first was from Labour North to thank me for my personal effort in the campaign. I had been proud to have played my part, of course. As Derek Foster's constituency secretary I'd been on the streets campaigning with a vibrant team of Party members ensuring that Bishop Auckland retained its status as a Labour stronghold. But I was truly astonished at the number of ordinary folk who knew me as their county councillor telephoning to share their own sense of joy that what some referred to as the 'evil of the tories' was, for now, dead and buried.

Possessing a wealth of experience as a Member of Parliament many people expected Derek Foster to be given a notable cabinet position in the Blair government. Derek had carried out his duties as opposition Chief Whip with a firm hand and had been steadfastly loyal to all Labour leaders since first elected in 1979. His political nous and intellect is renowned and his Keynsian thinking was well suited to his left wing ideology. Indeed, some Party members believe Derek had worked assiduously in Westminster specifically for the day when cabinet status might be attained. However, as that first victorious day wore on and each portfolio was filled, it became increasingly apparent that there would be no notable cabinet rank bestowed on Derek. A fair few in the Party were surprised. Derek more so, citing what he believed had been an earlier promise given to him by Tony Blair himself.

Derek was in fact given the cabinet post of Minister Of State but it fell far short of his expectations. Consequently, in post for just two days he called the television media to a briefing outside Parliament and announced publicly that he could not continue and would, instead, leave the job and sit as a backbench MP. At once he became highly critical of Tony Blair never missing an opportunity to speak out. Derek exacted revenge of sorts when he was later appointed chair of the Commons' select committee on employment. He used the post to openly criticise government policy before losing the chairmanship in 2001.

I had some sympathy for Derek and I went to see Alan Milburn, newly elected MP for Darlington and a close ally of Tony Blair. Alan's office was next door to where I worked at Royal Mail and I had organised the Darlington branch of the CWU to assist with Alan's own election campaign. He and I know each other well and I felt I could trust him in pitching for Derek. I explained I was concerned for Derek who held the view that Tony Blair had broken a promise. Whether a promise had actually been made or not, I really don't know, but I asked Alan if he would speak with Tony as a friend, relay to him my views, and perhaps get him to consider placing Derek in the House of Lords if there was never going to be a chance of a notable cabinet position.

"But why the hell should he?" was Alan's abrupt response.

Beyond offering words such as experience and loyalty, I didn't see any point in pressing further. Instead I left shortly after and telephoned Tony's constituency office leaving a message for his agent, John Burton, asking him to give me a call. There was no immediate response and I resigned myself to the belief that I was now being ignored. But then, some two or three weeks later, John called me at home.

"Can you come along to the office sometime, Phil? I need to speak to you about a couple of things."

167

Passing through armed security at Myrobella House in Trimdon I was ushered into Tony's office. There was no sign of Tony, only John who as always was friendly, upbeat and filled with his natural humour as we shook hands. Like me, John is a singer and musician who a few years earlier with The Scratch Band, and myself performing solo, had raised funds for striking firemen by hosting a concert for them in Spennymoor.

Coffee was served and John's demeanour changed. He began by telling me of Tony's discomfort at Derek's public pronouncements criticising the New Labour government. I told him that I was aware of Derek being upset, angry even, and that like others I had anticipated some cabinet portfolio for him in return for years of support and loyalty. I was not expecting to hear what John said next.

"Tony has asked me to get you in here, Phil. '*Get me Phil Graham*', he said."

"Why. What's up?"

"Would you be interested in the Bishop Auckland seat, Phil?"

I didn't reply and John went on...

"Tony wants Derek out of the way and is considering a seat for him in the House of Lords. He then wants you in the seat at Bishop because he knows he can trust you!"

Well. That came as something of a surprise.

168

My meeting with John, lasting much longer than the above brief transcript, was to be treated with all confidence, of course. And for good reason. Apart from confiding in Janet and my mother, this is honestly the first time I have openly recalled this particular episode and, I have no doubt, there may be moves by some to deny it ever took place. That's fine and is probably to be expected. However, twenty three years have passed and I feel comfortable relaying the general gist...if not the full detail.

Derek was eventually sent to the House of Lords in June 2005 to wear his ermine with the title, "Lord Foster of Auckland". As for myself and the Bishop Auckland seat? That went no further. *Quelle surprise…*

There is a sad footnote to the above… as I continued to research and write this book Derek Foster died aged 81 on Sunday 6th January 2019.

With increasing tension between Royal Mail and the CWU my role as branch secretary was now becoming more demanding. Advising and supporting workplace representatives alongside the area representatives had always been par for the course but now I found myself increasingly countering Royal Mail missives and a host of other local and national publications. I was often responding to quite blatant Royal Mail propaganda at the same time as ensuring the union's views were widely publicised. To assist me my fellow branch officials published a monthly newsletter called Grapevine.

Grapevine went out to union branches in newspaper format and it really got up the noses of some managers for its openness in exposing some of the guff coming down the line from the employer. In essence Grapevine reversed blind, authoritative management messages into the union's opposing view. I knew we were doing okay when we were awarded third place for content, layout and design in a national competition judged by a panel of designers and journalists in London.

There was a humorous element to Grapevine however and we'd always run a competition or print an entertaining article not necessarily concerned with industrial or political matters. One such article showed just how uptight a number of managers had become in discrediting the union in pressing home to our members an agenda which had little by way of maintaining, let alone improving, service to the public. Peter Woodend, our Area Processing Representative, wrote an article covering a Royal Mail initiative where workers were to be placed into teams headed by 'leaders' with every member of the team assuming joint and collective responsibility for outcomes within a particular work (or team) area. Competition between teams was to be encouraged and any slackers affecting results would be named and shamed. Teams, we were told, would also not need input from the union as issues would be identified and resolved within. The impudent arrogance was astonishing and anathema to good industrial relations.

Peter wrote, *"...and the next thing that is giving managers' orgasms is Team Working."* Within hours of publication I was summoned to the Area Manager's office.

The area manager at the time was Tony Fox. I liked Tony. He was a former professional footballer who also took an interest in my activities as a photographer. We generally got along. He was entirely business driven but often displayed his lighter side in private conversations we had. We afforded each other mutual respect in spite of many pressures from those who ruled above us. Having said that, he once told me he had planned to sack me for publishing a triptych of images in Grapevine – the cartoon character, Homer Simpson, Richmond MP William Hague and Tony Fox himself – with the invitation to readers to name the true Homer Simpson. That I'd been away on holiday at the time of publication had, apparently, granted him time to consider that the joke was precisely that... a joke. Anyway, back to the Peter Woodend article. Tony invited me to take a seat opposite him at his desk where he sat side by side with his operations manager who must remain anonymous here.

"What is the meaning of this?" Tony asked as he shuffled the magazine towards me.

"What? Which bit are you referring to this month?" I sighed scanning the offered page for a clue.

"That bit about team working and orgasms," he pointed to the headline.

"That's not my article," I said. "And besides, what on earth is wrong with it? It's Peter's way of injecting a bit of humour. Are we heading towards censorship, here?"

Tony's Ops Manager then piped up telling me that he had found the article offensive and that so had a number of female employees. I knew from feedback received that that was a load of bollocks.

"Give over," I scoffed. "I've had nobody complain to me about it and, come on, guys it's meant to be fun. Orgasms are fun."

I swear what happened next will live with me till the day I die. The Ops Manager leaned forward, stared me in the eye and said... "They are not funny when you haven't had one for a while!"

I burst out laughing. I then saw that neither of my inquisitors were laughing. I wondered if I was being subjected to a joke and that the punch line was about to be delivered. When it wasn't I stood up, said something about not being so stupid and walked out.

During the summer of 1997 I embarked upon a programme of visits to meet with groups of CWU members away from their place of work after the end of their shifts; usually early to mid afternoon. The idea was to engage openly about current issues and to listen to concerns and queries and to answer any questions. In the main the visits proved useful and I had planned one a week visiting Spennymoor, Bishop Auckland, Newton Aycliffe, Bedale, Richmond, Barnard Castle, Northallerton and Leyburn. Not only were they helpful to me in explaining current CWU policies and campaigning positions away from the ever distrustful eyes and ears of managers but members were pleased to 'put a face to the name' while taking advantage of asking some quite probing questions.

It was during a visit to Leyburn, a delightfully located delivery office in rural North Yorkshire, that I began to feel unwell. In the middle of my report to members my chest began to feel compressed and I found it increasingly hard to breathe. What I can only describe as a tingling rush seared up the left side of my body and my sight became blurred. I felt as if I was going to faint. Stupidly, assuming the feelings would quickly pass, I carried on speaking and my legs gave way. I don't think I fell unconsciousness and I recovered my composure sufficiently to apologise and announce my intention to leave.

Driving through Darlington on my way home the tingling rush came again. I pulled over and, once parked, I went into a full blown panic. Convinced I was having a stroke or maybe the onset of a heart attack I stepped out of the car and hurriedly crossed the road to the house of a postwoman I knew. Deliah Carvey lived in the Faverdale area of town but she wasn't at home when I called. My heart sank and the pressure in my chest increased as I knocked furiously on her door. I really was in a state of panic by now and I got back in the car and drove for home some ten miles away. Approaching the junction of the A68 flyover over the A1M motorway I was relieved to see a parked police patrol car. I pulled over, got out and ran blindly to the passenger door begging the policeman inside for help and then I collapsed into the passenger seat.

When I came to I was in an ambulance. Judging it prudent to lie still and allow my surroundings to come into focus, I tried to answer a series of calmly offered questions. I could only mumble in response. Yet in spite of my concerns an air of professionalism among those who were dealing with me had a profoundly calming effect.

I was fully conscious when I arrived at Darlington Memorial Hospital and was experiencing none of the discomfort from earlier. A series of inconclusive tests followed before I was eventually despatched to a ward to be 'kept under observation'. A nurse who I came to know as Joanna greeted me and said she'd be looking after me till they could find out was wrong. Her calmness was reassuring and I gave her Janet's details requesting that she be told where I was. Joanna then set about attaching me to an ECG machine and inserted a canular into a vein in my left hand. Handing me an alarm buzzer, I was advised to lie still and relax and that someone would be in to see me shortly.

Thankfully, every ensuing examination confirmed I had not suffered a stroke nor had I had a heart attack and I was sent home within a few days replete with a sick note absenting me from work for two weeks. However, what had caused me to collapse had yet to ascertained and I was given an appointment to return to see a consultant whose surname is all I can recall – Connolly. Mister Connolly, to give due deference to his elevated status in the NHS, referred me to the gym in the physio department where, wired once again to an ECG machine, I was shown to a treadmill. After a brief explanation about what was going to happen I was handed a clear plastic breathing tube to insert in my mouth the other end of which passed through the rear of a nearby monitor where my oxygen levels and heart rate were to be recorded.

At first the treadmill speed was set to barely walking pace and I quickly relaxed into the exercise. Easy peasy, I thought. Then the pace began to quicken. Brisker steps led to jogging and then moderate running. I was doing alright, though, and I concentrated on my breathing. In truth a more accurate description of my breathing would be *puffing and panting, gasping for breath and a lot of obscene grunting and snorting.* And just as my legs were starting to tire the

175

buggers tilted the treadmill to simulate running uphill. Now it was getting serious. Some twenty minutes passed during which I became soaked with sweat and was never so pleased to feel things slowing down and eventually stop. Exhausted and with wobbly legs I was invited to relax and cool down before being sent home with a further appointment to return the following week.

The first few minutes of my second visit with Mr.Connolly were conversational. He enquired about my life, work and interests and asked me to describe how I had been feeling over the past few months. I told him that I had been okay in general but with the pressure from competing demands I acknowledged that I had let personal health and wellbeing slip somewhat. He probed my alcohol consumption – moderate to heavy! Diet – okay at home, not okay away from home! Exercise – practically non-existent after years of hillwalking, cycling and tennis! Smoking – no! Weight – burgeoning. I was comfortable enough in his company to admit that I was more tired than usual and often had difficulty sleeping. In addition I opened up about having become irritable and impatient, quick to temper and that I kept hidden from family and friends bouts of anxiety and foreboding.

"Let's make a list of everything you do, Philip", he suggested.

He jotted down as I recalled…postal worker, trade union official, branch political officer, regional committee delegate, constituency Labour Party secretary, county councillor, vice chair Environment Scrutiny Committee, Labour North Regional Executive member, delegate to the European Labour Party, delegate to Wear Valley District Labour Party, school governor, photographer, musician.

The room fell silent as he slowly ran his pen up and down the list after I had finished.

"Hmmm. Are you sure this is all, Philip?"

"That's about it as far I know."

"You're absolutely sure there's nothing else?"

"Nope. There's nothing else I can think of."

What he said next rocked me…

"What about husband and father?"

It was as if I'd been slapped across my face and I was stunned to my very core. With all that I had going on in and around my life it now dawned in a blinding flash of light that I was actually giving more and more of myself to others and less and less to those who really matter – my family. This sudden realisation proved too much and a wave of unstoppable emotion took over. Embarrassed and ashamed by the unexpected epiphany, I broke down in tears.

Connolly remained unmoved by the scene unfolding before his eyes and, beyond calling for a nurse to bring a glass of water, he offered no solace. He stared at me over half rimmed glasses as I began to take control again.

"I think, perhaps, you understand now", he said. "What you experienced a couple of weeks ago was a classic case of your body sending out a warning. You have been doing too much for too long. Take heed, Philip. Ease off the pace...or else!"

My two weeks sick note was extended to three months.

9 – Onwards and Downwards

Janet was well known throughout the area in which we lived. During her daily routine walking Daniel and Padraic to Coundon Primary School, returning home and going back again to collect them in the afternoon, she would stop and chat with people she met along the way. From these passing conversations she would deliver news and messages to me about local concerns and community issues at the same time as strengthening her own presence and friendships.

She took a job as a supervisory assistant at the school - the role was colloquially referred to as 'dinner nanny' - where her rapport with the children, staff and parents added to her growing circle of friends and acquaintances. Additionally, she was popularly known for her role in the local Labour Party and for her support for myself and my fellow Coundon councillors. It came as no surprise then when she was selected to stand for the Coundon seat on Wear Valley District Council which she won on Thursday 6th May 1999. I was thrilled and so proud of her. Janet proved a popular and hardworking councillor dealing with peoples queries and concerns as she went about her daily domestic routines.

Being the youngest of the female councillors, she often felt frustration over what she regarded as the older 'stuck in their ways' women with whom she worked alongside on committees. As evidenced when I was first elected twelve years earlier, some of the old guard didn't always warm to new faces who brought youthfulness, ideas and energy. There was a way of doing things that should not be challenged or questioned. The status quo must prevail. That's fair enough where procedural and constitutional matters are concerned but discussing ideas and policy? Nah!

She got on well with the council's officers, many of whom politely tolerated less courteous councillors from all political sides of whom some were prone to table-thumping their demands. Janet adopted the manner of her more polite colleagues and was more measured in her approach. She rightly respected council officers as professionals who were there to help, advise and support individuals and political group policies.

I was proud of her. For someone who had moved from her family home in Lancashire and had become a mother, a wife and a person of some regard in the community all in the space of just fifteen years, in the eyes of many who came to know her she stood out as a remarkably talented and considerate woman. Never one for seeking praise for herself, with the exception of her familial achievements, she received sparse acknowledgement of her political and vocational competencies from our respective families.

Throughout my own life I have been somewhat at odds with the aspirations of my family. My ideas, beliefs, politics, music and writing were often seen as just another fad. That these fads brought varying degrees of local, regional and national recognition and have led me to where I am today, they nevertheless drew what I always felt was scant regard from my brother, my mother and my stepfather.

Janet remained similarly unsung. From her own family and friends in Lancashire, loving, caring and supportive as is their nature, there was little said of her political and community achievements here in County Durham. From relative obscurity as a child and teenager to becoming a district councillor overseeing inward investment, business and leisure developments for industry, residents and communities, as well as becoming chair of the council's Licensing Sub Committee, I was immensely proud of her.

There was, however, one noteworthy civic occasion which captured the full attention of my mother. A staunch monarchist she always said that if I ever received an invitation to a royal event she would expect to attend as my partner. Protocols abound in such circumstances and royal invitations to partners and consorts are determined by marital status. Whether it's the same today I have no idea but as the world slipped into the new millennium it was basically this - for husbands it is his wife who attends and for a bachelor the accepted partner is his mother. If the wife or

181

mother is no longer alive, a sister is permitted to attend and so on. The same gender profiles apply to women invitees who would attend with male relatives.

Well, imagine my surprise when in April 2000 myself and fellow county councillor, Len O'Donnell, received invitations to Her Majesty The Queen's Garden Party at Buckingham Palace. The royal event was scheduled for 22nd June. Now, I am quite ambivalent where matters of the royal family are concerned. I neither love 'em nor loath 'em. I have, however, studied English history and have a fascination for the barbarism, disloyalty, infidelities, disputes, trials and tribulations which have created what we call the monarchy. I was delighted and honoured, therefore, to accept the invitation.

Rather than being pleased for me my mother was, to put it mildly, crestfallen. Janet and I were married by this time and that meant my mother was not eligible to attend. She hid her disappointment to some extent but Janet and I sensed the silent curses and metaphorical poisoned daggers being hurled in our direction.

Also around this time changes were taking place in the upper echelons of the CWU with Billy Hayes elected to the post of General Secretary in May 2001. A dedicated and relentless branch representative from Liverpool before becoming a member of the union's executive council, Billy was a passionate speaker in conference debates quickly and effectively slipping into the role of a thoughtful and diligent leader. The same age as me, we share many cultural, music and literary interests.

One very late evening in the bar of the union's Elstead Hotel in Bournemouth, I was playing a guitar and singing Stephen Stills' song, Four and Twenty. Although a classic, my rendition was but minor entertainment to those not too drunk to listen. Billy knew, though. He understood the meaning, the story, the sense of loss running through the piece. Like myself he listens to music beyond the puerile confines of popular radio.

Billy was later followed by Dave Ward from Lambeth, a fellow musician who plays blues guitar and who had been an executive council member before becoming Outdoor Secretary in 2001. Dave was elected Deputy General Secretary in 2003 and, in 2015, went on to beat Billy in a ballot for the ultimate prize – that of General Secretary.

During Billy's tenure, however, the union developed a more robust Political Organising Department. The department's remit included encouraging and training CWU members who were also members of the Labour Party to stand for Parliament, thereby ensuring CWU policies were placed at the heart of UK democracy and decision making. Headed by the affable Derek Bourne, applications were sought from interested members to be considered for

183

inclusion on the union's Parliamentary panel. The invitation to apply was published in a weekly Branch Officials Bulletin (BOB), a multi paragraph missive covering all industrial sectors pertaining to the union, as well as in a Letter To Branches (LTB) a focussed, single topic paragraph or two. I was only mildly interested at first until a number of colleagues suggested I put my name forward. Didn't I have enough to do already? That was the question I asked myself and in discussions with Janet. A number of colleagues from the region were also supportive of the idea pointing out my established role within the Labour Party both locally and regionally. I was persuaded that it would be a natural progression enabling me, if successful, to bring together my trade union and political interests.

The selection of panellists took place in the union's education centre in the grand environs of Alvescot Lodge in rural west Oxfordshire. Situated adjacent to RAF Brize Norton there was little distraction for students save for a small pub in the nearby village. It was the perfect setting for undisturbed education and training. Alvescot Lodge had a uniquely consequential reputation for student punctuality at breakfast. Due to the close proximity of the airfield and, with the runway ending just yards away from our sleeping quarters, a daily six o'clock in the morning take off of heavy and noisy military aircraft lifting to the sky just above our heads, meant sleeping in was not possible. Great fun. Not.

I arrived at Alvescot with John Fairclough who represented CWU members in Girobank in Bootle (now Alliance & Leicester plc). John and I met up by chance at Birmingham New Street railway station from where, following an announcement of a severely delayed connection to Oxford, I telephoned Derek Bourne to explain I would be arriving late.

"Don't worry, Phil", said Derek. "I've just had a call from a fella on his way down from Liverpool telling me the same thing. His name is John. John Fairclough. Get the station to put out a call for him and see if you can come in together on the next train and then share a taxi from Oxford."

"Would Mister John Fairclough travelling to Oxford please report to the passenger information desk. Would Mister John Fairclough travelling to Oxford please report to the passenger information desk."

Hoping that John would hear the announcement I waited in the passenger lounge with a cup of coffee. Having never met before I had no idea what he looked like so I asked the attendant to point him out to me when he arrived. And what an arrival. Upon hearing the announcement John had feared the worst. *What's happened? Had someone been hurt at home, perhaps?* As soon as I heard the worried scouse accent speaking anxiously to the reassuring attendant, I knew it was John. I introduced myself and we shook hands, exchanged greetings and names, cracked a joke about the current situation we found ourselves in and have been friends ever since. In the years to follow Janet and myself would attend John's fiftieth birthday celebrations and he and I would meet up whenever our CWU roles brought us together at annual conferences and such.

John and I formed part of a group of ten selected for training to the Parliamentary Panel. The training sessions over the next few months gave us all a thorough grounding in presentation, appearance, handling the press (journalists from ITV and BBC put us through our paces here), appearing on television, radio and in newspapers and a whole host of media techniques designed to stave off the inevitable scrutiny should we ever become MP's.

My first subsequent attempt at a seat was Sheffield Heeley where Bill Michie had announced he was to retire. My chances of replacing Bill were slim from the outset with my being unknown *and* an outsider. It was invaluable experience, though. Derek Bourne arranged for me to meet Bill in the House of Commons to get to know all about the Heeley constituency and what mattered there and what did not. A later meeting over lunch with CWU sponsored Derby South MP, Bob Laxton proved useful in terms of getting to know the workings of Parliament and individual members roles and input. In addition, my friend, Mick Dunlavey, Political Officer for the CWU South Yorkshire branch took

186

me under his wing and showed me around the constituency, even to the point of arranging an overnight stay for Janet and myself in the Leeds Hilton where a regional Labour Party dinner had been scheduled. In the end the Sheffield Party selected local candidate, Meg Munn, who went on to win and hold the seat till March 2015.

A little later I was advised that Giles Radice was going to retire from Chester Le Street. Being only sixteen or so miles from Bishop Auckland it seemed perfect for me to throw my hat in the ring to replace him. Alas, this is where I received a full smack in the face of what can go wrong when sections of the same organisation do not liaise effectively. The call to apply for selection to Chester le Street came from the Political Organising department in CWU headquarters. However, as soon as my application had been submitted I was contacted by Dorothy Burnett, a personal friend and CWU National Officer and stalwart of many years standing and who lived in the north east region. Dorothy was alarmed to have heard about my application.

"Phil, man", she began. "What are you doing? Kevan Jones from the GMB has had Chester le Street earmarked for years and we are supporting him. I wouldn't go there if I were you, pet." I didn't. Kevan has been the Member of Parliament for Chester le Street ever since.

Then Peter Mandelson announced his retirement in Hartlepool. This time I was ready. Following a thorough vetting and interview the Party chose myself and local man Ian Wright along with Lee Vasey, a councillor from Darlington to face the local members to determine which of us would contest the seat. The stage was set. Wiser now and better prepared I really did sail with ease through the selection process following some extensive research and networking. In the run up to the selection meeting, and because of the high profile nature of Peter Mandelson and the Hartlepool seat, the three of us were photographed by the press in and around the town and each of us garnered support from a number of local Party activists

On the evening of the selection meeting I gave a measured and carefully worded speech before answering a series of questions. I felt I had convinced the members of Hartlepool CLP that I should be their next general election candidate. The members, not all by any means, but a majority nevertheless went for local man, Ian Wright.

Time and circumstance would prevent me attempting further seats but I value the experience and opportunities which had been afforded me.

As a Parliamentary panellist I was often invited by my union to attend political workshops, briefings and conferences. At these I got to know a number of Labour MP's and government ministers some of whom I built strong and influential friendships. And although I had been to a number Labour Party conferences – my first was to

Blackpool in 1992 as a delegate from Bishop Auckland CLP and at which I spoke in the Education debate – I now found myself representing the CWU either as a visitor or, more frequently as an accredited delegate.

These major political conferences provided plenty of opportunity to extend my network of notable people and I milked it for all it was worth. In addition to many Labour MP's (and some tories) and ministers I was also privileged to meet with the likes of The Queen, Prince Charles, Princess Ann, President Bill Clinton; one more open and friendly than the other – but I shalln't say who. I can also vainly count a raft of so called celebrities from the international world of arts, film and entertainment – the actors Tony Booth from the classic British television sitcom 'Till Death Us Do Part' and American film icon, Kevin Spacey, were among the most notable. Controversially, to some at least, I shared lunch alongside IRA commander, Martin McGuinness, prior to a conference fringe meeting on Irish peace initiatives. I was taken by his gentle and quiet persona. Heady times indeed. My contact book of MP's, Ministers and others grew and grew.

My photographic role with Bishop Auckland Football Club began by chance in 2002. I received a call from one of the directors seeking a photographer to record the last ever match at their historically famous ground on Kingsway. It was a sad yet splendid occasion with our MP, Derek Foster, in attendance along with a number of surviving club luminaries from the "Glory Years" of the 1950's when Bishop Auckland FC were known the world over. The match was played against Bradford Park Avenue who went on to win 4 – 2.

My brief was to photograph not just the match but also the ground itself including the terraces, the main stand, changing rooms and supporters – anything in fact that would eventually succumb to a developer's JCB to make way for a sheltered housing complex.

As a result of that brief I am the only person with a full historic record of that special day. Of course local press photographers were there too but they only took pictures of the actual match. My pictures went on display in the town's Discovery Centre and are now archived as an historic record at County Hall in Durham. I retain full copyright of all the images and have all the negatives along with digital files and CD's. A montage of some of my photos hangs in The Colin Rowell Suite at the club's impressive new ground at Heritage Park.

The directors and supporters really appreciated what I had done and I developed a relationship with many including the then chairman, Terry Jackson. It was Terry who went on to steer the development of the new ground after years of sharing with nearby Shildon and West Auckland Football

Clubs. I started attending matches and submitted my photos to local newspapers along with brief reports and eventually, and without any formal negotiation, I became the club's official photographer and joined the Supporters Club. In turn I am also a shareholder with the club.

I am a firm believer in forging relationships and it is through my association with the football club and, in particular my friendship with Terry, that in 2018 I was chosen to be presented with a cheque to the value of one thousand pounds on behalf of the Guillain Barre & Associated Inflammatory Neuropathies charity (GAIN).

This rather welcome largesse came from now retired Northern Echo journalist, Mike Amos, former chairman of the Northern League and font of all things football. Mike had raised twenty eight thousand pounds walking to each of the forty five northern league football grounds. It was his Last Legs Challenge and he donated half of the money to The Sir Bobby Robson Foundation and the rest to each of the football clubs. When Bishop Auckland Football Club was approached to name their cause or charity they came up with GAIN - and who better to receive the cheque for them? Yes. Me.

In March 2003 the Communication Workers Union North East Regional Secretary, Brian Cassidy, retired. A senior officer with the Sheffield postal branch, this straight talking

Glaswegian had made me welcome when I attended my first regional committee meeting some years before.

I warmed to him straight away and sensed from the outset that he was well liked amongst fellow delegates. Brian had an unshakeable belief in and loyalty towards the 'family' which was our trade union. Gruff in conversation, steely eyed and with a seasoned and lined face suggesting a no-nonsense approach to life and business, he could be a formidable presence in company. Yet I always considered that he disguised a certain lack of intellect behind the hard persona. He wasn't the most astute thinker I have ever met and he was prone to outbursts of unvalidated protestation which were either modified soon after or, more usually, quietly forgotten.

Here was a man, a most likeable character, who was used to speaking first and considering later. Brian's main interest away from the union was his grandchildren and, when announcing his intention to retire, he cited spending more time with them as a major consideration. His softer side shone through when he spoke of them and after his retirement speech in York's Post Office Club and following post-meeting drinks, of which there was plenty, I wished him well and watched as he strode away alone to the railway station. I never heard of him nor saw him again.

10 - Back To Face The Music

I gave up live performing when I became a father in 1986. My priorities changed and something had to give way in order for me to continue with a growing workload in the trade union and in politics. My work as a photographer also eased to the point of only accepting commissions for family and friends. Playing guitar and singing were similarly limited to family parties and close friend social events. For the next few years I immersed myself in the Labour Party, the union and in my role as a county councillor and as a father, first to Daniel and later in 1990 to Padraic. It was a most wonderful period in my life and Janet and I are today blessed with having two grown up, well rounded and settled sons the result, we dare claim, of our devotion and care as young parents.

Enter Graeme Carroll in January 2004. I knew Graeme from Wear Valley District Council, he was a council officer when I was a councillor there between 1987 and 1991. Graeme was also one half of popular acoustic duo, Brother Crow, where he and his co-partner, Andy Davison, would be seen at festivals and folk clubs round and about. They had a loyal following and had produced a couple of CD's which were on general release. For anyone who has enjoyed or endured my revived live performances since January 2004, you have Graeme Carroll to thank… or blame.

"Why don't you come along to Croxdale one night?" he asked.

"The folk club?" I replied derisorily. "I'm not a folk singer."

"I know! You don't need to be. We have all kinds of music and musicians. Come along and see for yourself."

I'm pleased I did go along and see. The Folk Club meets in The Daleside Inn in Croxdale, a former mining village north east of Spennymoor, and it was there that I met a most friendly bunch of people, mainly musicians, though some non-playing locals also who had come along to listen. Graeme introduced me to the likes of Chris Milner, Marie Little, Bert Draycott, The Old Aged Travellers, jiva and Fred Brierley to name a few. I was warmly welcomed and I watched and listened intently whilst waiting for my turn to play. Being a debut I elected not to play my own songs. Instead, if my memory prevails, I sang Jimmy MacCarthy's, Missing You, in the style of Christy Moore, both of whom are folk heroes of mine. For my second song I chose a traditional Irish/Australian ballad, The Wild Colonial Boy.

And that's how it all began again. With Daniel now seventeen and Padraic thirteen, I went along to The Daleside Inn most Tuesday fortnights from where I eventually branched out to play folk clubs and festivals across Durham, Teesside and Yorkshire.

Coming from a rock and roll background I felt it prudent to modify my delivery of songs and make them *folk-accessible* to my newfound venues and audiences. There are a number of purists on the folk circuit; not quite woolly jumpers and fingers in ears but doggedly and sincerely engaged in "keeping alive the tradition" not just of music but poetry, stories and dance. I recall my first visit to The Woodman Inn near Bedale where, sharing the evening with established folk performers and, following a set of some six or seven songs, I was only mildly applauded when event organiser, Paul Arrowsmith, declared, *"And there we have Phil Graham reminding us of his rock and roll roots!"* I'm not entirely sure if he was being complimentary. I suspect he wasn't.

Which brings me to a note about the people I was now associating with and performing to. The vast majority are wonderful beings, knowledgeable about the music and oh so very welcoming. One or two, though, extended only polite courtesies, barely tolerating this upstart newcomer who had invaded their circle with his barely disguised rock and roll influences. Importantly, I learned who had influence over which acts would most likely be selected to perform at festivals and the like. Get along with these people, I was advised, and a level of exposure and accessibility could be virtually guaranteed.

One of the most respected regional folk luminaries of the time was Fred Brierley. Born in 1932, Fred was kind, welcoming and bright as a button and one who regaled audiences with his vast catalogue of traditional songs and expert whistle playing. He was also a member of trad folk outfit, The Ancient Mariners. Indeed, Fred was involved in most things on the folk music circuit and, living just a few doors away from The Daleside Inn, was a regular presence there. Graeme Carroll had advised me early on "not to upset" Fred. He wasn't threatening me or being unfriendly. No, I was advised that Fred Brierley was so well liked, venerated even, that any sleight on his name or character would be felt by many musicians and loyal friends. I heeded Graeme's advice and when the annual Croxdale Traditional Music Festival came around in 2006 I bunged Fred two hundred pounds by way of sponsorship from my then part time business, FILMAR Photography. My fate as a friend of Fred's was thus sealed and I was given a slot at the festival taking the Saturday afternoon stage after jiva, The Young Un's and before Chris Milner. Sadly, Fred died in August 2012 but his legacy within northern folk music lives on.

In October 2007 I was offered a weekly 'stooge' role on Bishop FM Radio. My friend, Terry Ferdinand, hosted a popular Monday evening Folk Show and asked me to join him to banter with both himself and his listeners and engage with invited guest musicians. I also got to perform a couple of my own songs on air. Being an independent radio station the broadcast range isn't much more than about six miles. However, the internet brought in a listenership from many parts of the UK and as far away as South America, Africa and the USA. Terry, who died from the effects of an aggressive brain tumour in 2014, became something of a legend both locally and on the internet with hundreds of loyal fans listening in each week. The Folk Show is still broadcast today and is hosted by Rebekah Findlay and her partner, Lee Huck.

Looking back to 2002 I was invited to become a non-executive director of The Bishop Auckland Hospital NHS Trust. I know, I know… more strings!! From there, after a further two years, the Trust was subsumed into the supposedly more cost effective and operationally efficient, County Durham & Darlington NHS Hospitals Trust and where I was handed the Audit portfolio. It was a portfolio I was hopelessly unsuited to. Every organisation and business has its acronyms but the NHS has more than seven hundred and when I learned that SCBU referred to Special Care Baby Unit, ECAP was Emergency Care Action Plan and that ACAD was ambulatory care and diagnostic unit, I thought how easy it might be to learn Swahili.

Nevertheless, I was honoured to serve on the Bishop Auckland Trust along with my good friend, Nick Beddow, vicar of Escomb of whom I wrote in Chapter 6. Nick had by that time become wheelchair dependent due to Multiple Sclerosis and it irked him greatly to have severely limited freedom of mobility. Renowned for straight speaking, infrequent mild cursing and a scrutinising manner, his illness only served to augment his challenging presence in meetings. Nick didn't transfer to the new Trust and sadly died in 2008.

My past dealings with public bodies had weathered me against the lie that *"you'll only be required one or two days a month"*. Indeed, insofar as the County Durham & Darlington NHS Trust was concerned, I often found myself in meetings at least once a week and sometimes more. If it hadn't been for an arrangement between myself and Royal Mail Processing Manager, Kevin Harland, where in addition to nationally agreed special leave entitlements we drew up our own local agreement giving me time off every afternoon to deal with my union work and my many other public, civic and political roles, I don't think I could have carried on.

Kevin could be quite taciturn. Comradely, jokey and one of the lads one day and cheesed off, frustrated and a bit grumpy the next. One never quite knew what the mood and demeanour would be from one shift to the next. Having said that, in spite of what some managers referred to as my "taking the piss" in having so much leave away from work, Kevin was always approachable and generally understanding, if not always fully supportive, of my legitimate needs. I sensed that he was much relieved to be offered an early retirement package when it came in due course.

There were occasional attempts by a coterie of managers to undermine my ability to carry out non-Royal Mail activities. These usually arose in the form of pathetically incorrect mutterings amongst themselves about how much time I was spending on public and civic responsibilities. Once or twice such mutterings found their way to the then Area manager, Nick Morgan. Nick and I got on well and while he was supportive of his management teams, he saw through the froth of what some were trying to do in terms of their tittle tattle against me. And whereas Kevin Harland and I didn't see eye to eye all the time, for the most part we got on well as long as my weekly whereabouts sheet was duly filled out and left on his desk each previous Friday.

I had to face the music of a different kind on the morning November 4th 2004. Labour's deputy leader, John Prescott, had promised to deliver devolution of power to the north east and an autumn campaign was duly set up to deliver just that. Designed to give north east councils a higher degree of autonomy and a bigger say in a wide range of policies,

John's campaign naturally attracted nationwide coverage on television, radio and in the newspapers with Labour North officials and executive officers, myself included, at its heart. I sensed disaster long before the end of the campaign. It was clear to me, and to a fair few others if they were to be honest enough, that the electorate weren't particularly warm to the idea. Most, in spite of the plethora of campaign publicity, didn't fully understand what devolution meant and those that did were swayed more by the arguments against. The outcome for the Party was disastrous. Devolution, John Prescott's policy flagship at the time, was sunk without trace as the region voted firmly to reject the notion.

On the morning following the result we who had campaigned were summoned to Labour North Head Office where our deputy leader wished to address us. Coffee, tea and bacon sandwiches were gloomily taken while each of us in turn gave our account of where and why we thought the campaign had failed. John, clearly angry and somewhat embarrassed, had to face the press later and our synopses would form the foundation of his responses to their questions There was no easy way out for him, us or the Party. I have always liked John and I felt a degree of sympathy for him that morning, but the idea of devolution had singularly failed to inspire the public and the media were salivating. I was never more relieved to get in the car and drive home thankful that the whole bloody farce was now over.

But then, before the dust had settled on my role in the devolution fiasco, Bishop Auckland CLP was decreed an all women shortlist seat for the 2005 general election. Ironically, given the furore with which members had protested against the earlier imposition in 1997, castigating me in the process, this time around the policy was accepted without a fuss. Not a whimper. No resistance whatsoever. There you go, eh?!

I heard that one or two Party members had discussed what they understood were my feelings about the all women shortlist. I didn't respond. But let me now say this…it is true, yes, that I would have liked to have stood for selection to be Labour's general election candidate for Bishop Auckland. However, I never viewed that as a given or a right. Although I was well known throughout the towns and villages within the constituency and had given my all to the administration of the CLP and its members over ten years, this is where I need to set the record straight… I would have readily accepted defeat in an open selection process if that had been the will of the members, but to not have had the chance to 'give it a go' is what irked me. For some to suggest that I 'spat out my dummy' and resigned from the role of CLP secretary in pique, is so very wrong and wide of the mark. When Helen Goodman was subsequently selected to be the candidate it was obvious to me quite early on that she had different ideas about how she wanted the constituency to be run. Her management of people, particularly those who came to work or volunteer for her, was demanding from the outset, unnecessarily abrupt and, at times, quite rude. I felt the time was prudent to stand down as secretary and encourage someone else to come forward. Simple as. No hard feelings whatsoever.

I came to the attention of the media again in May 2007. This time because of my refusal to accept a Local Government Pay Body Review recommending a rise in allowances for councillors. I was astonished to think we were about to accept additional allowances for ourselves when our communities, families and individuals were crying out for all manner of services and support. Now, I have absolutely no objection to remunerating councillors. The job is voluntary and subject to the whims of voters, or at least the whims of those who can actually be bothered to vote, but it is also virtually 24/7 and for those councillors who have jobs and who lose pay to attend to their civic roles, the amount we were receiving back in 2007 barely covered the losses. I was fortunate in that Royal Mail granted me paid leave up to a specified number of days per year.

I was joined in my opposition to the proposed rise by fellow Labour councillor, Paul Trippet and because of our persistence in speaking out against the recommendation we were called before the Whips and Labour Group leaders to be advised that we had to accept the rise if the majority in

202

the Labour group voted for it. To do otherwise, we were warned, could lead to us both having the whip removed necessitating in us having to continue as Independent councillors with no access nor input into the Labour Group. I can't recall what Paul's response was but I am certain it was along similar lines to mine…

"Okay. Impose it if you will. But I shall donate mine each month to Coundon & Leeholme Community Partnership!"

And so I did. On the last day of every month I personally visited the offices of the Partnership on Tees Walk in Coundon and wrote out a cheque for them to the sum of whatever additional remuneration I had been paid. So did Paul; although his went to a beneficiary in his own Trimdon ward. The Coundon & Leeholme Community Partnership were delighted and the press were salivating once again. Overnight, when the news of our rebellion broke, Paul and I became heroes of our communities as the Northern Echo and local tv and radio reported on our defiant use of the additional largesse.

In spite of a range of successes and accomplishments I was now beginning to lose drive, commitment, ideas and energy. Increasingly missing out on good night sleeps, my drinking was also getting out of hand and a combination of the two meant I was constantly tired. My mind occasionally wandered back to the time a few years earlier when I had taken several weeks off on sick leave due to stress. I did not want a repeat of that situation.

Royal Mail let it be known they were seeking to voluntary retire some 40,000 staff and I had indicated I'd be happy to consider the option whenever and if it might be confirmed. Around that same time Janet and I decided that I should stand again in the county council elections in May 2008 and if re-elected, make that my last four year term. Doing so would mean that, by the subsequent election in May 2012, I would have been a councillor for twenty five years. Some achievement. Additionally, should an early voluntary retirement package be offered we calculated that it would most likely come on or around my fifty fifth birthday in August of 2008, If so, and dependent upon favourable terms, we agreed that I should accept it. The future for FILMAR Photography and my music would be subject to subsequent future discussion.

11 – After All These Years

The Phoenix Club in Newton Aycliffe on St.Patrick's Day is a wondrous place to be. Known as The Royal British Legion Club before disaffiliating and rebranding in 2015, the Phoenix is renowned for comfortable lounges, three bars, a restaurant and first rate entertainment. On 17th March every year, no matter what day that happens to fall, the club's members take on the wildest excesses of the emerald isle and the craic becomes mighty indeed. Guinness, whiskey and all manner of looney soups flow through the long mad day with non-Irish men and women made up and dressed as plastic paddies alongside a handful of genuine article Irish ex-pats. To soak up the drink there is food, karaoke, bingo, disco and live entertainment.

This annual gaelfest always intrigued me, particularly when one considers the historical conflicts between British military and the many men and women of Ireland taking a stance against what they saw as a foreign invasion. But who gives a damn about that here on the mainland? This is for fun. This is heaven and this is hell. 'Two more pints of Guinness, please.' In 2008, when the club was still the Legion, I wrote to Irish music legend, Christy Moore, telling him I was booked to perform there and how I looked forward to it as each year rolled around. I mentioned my Irish descendancy and asked him if he had any messages to convey to the committee and the members.

"Have a good time", he pointedly replied. "But I'm not ready to play best friends yet."

I have played around fifteen 'Paddy' shows for the club over twenty five years or so, never once taking payment for my efforts save for a handful of free drinks tokens. They were solo shows mainly, just me and a guitar, four were with full bands and one as a trio where I took no payment but made sure the other musicians were paid. I did these shows freely because my late uncle, Irishman Eddie Graham, was an active club member, a committee man and, in his later years, the club's chairman. Never once, though, was I ever invited back to perform for an actual fee at any other events. For all that, I love them still.

So how did the family connection between County Antrim and County Durham come about? Well... Sam Graham, my father, along with his brothers Eddie and Bobby, was born in Ballynure to Robert Graham and Sadie McNally; a controversial coupling at the time with Robert a protestant and Sadie from catholic stock. Sadie died aged just 32 after which Robert and his three sons, moved to Bishop Auckland in 1945 where he was stationed as a soldier in the British army.

For the St.Patrick's Day show in 2008 I asked Gary Grainger, then a county council officer acquaintance, to join me in providing additional vocals and second guitar. I'd known Gary for a couple of years, not just with the council but as a fine guitar player who can adapt to any genre. He had also played acoustic and slide guitars on my second album, Strange Kind Of Way. Gary asked if he could bring a friend along to play with us. To be honest I wasn't keen on the idea but when he mentioned that his friend was an accomplished drummer who played bodhran, cajon and whistles, I saw the potential for a rousing set of Irish songs and tunes. Enter David Pratt from Richmond in North Yorkshire. The three of us had time for only one rehearsal and yet the show was a runaway success. We stayed together for a couple of years playing a series of shows around the region under the name Tri, the Irish for three. Gary left in 2010 and David and I brought in Ken Robinson on guitar and Steve Eliffe on fiddle and mandolin. We changed our name to Dead Cat Bounce, soon to be dropped after hearing of an already successful outfit of the same name touring Asia at the time. Dead Cat Bounce then became Man With The Stick.

My plan to serve one last term as a county councillor was dashed when I lost my seat in the 2008 elections. Chris Foote-Wood had taken local residents Dorothy Burn and Tommy Taylor under his wing and persuaded them to join the Lib-Dems and stand as election candidates. I knew

Dorothy through my public engagements and as a school governor in the area where she lived in Coundon Grange. I felt she was typical of many who often had something to complain about whilst offering little by way of workable solutions. Nonetheless, I liked her and our relationship was always polite and cordial. As regards, Tommy? Well, he was a decent man, a former amateur boxer and with many friends in and around Coundon. I didn't consider either he nor Dorothy as serious election contenders, however. That turned out to be a big mistake. With Chris Foote-Wood as their election agent they fought a bruising campaign keeping fellow Labour candidate Neil Stonehouse and myself on our toes. With the addition of two conservative candidates the campaign was a classic three way contest.

On the evening of Thursday 1st May in Willington's Spectrum Leisure Centre the returning officer announced the result: T Taylor (Liberal Democrat) 669 votes, D Burn (Liberal Democrat) 634 votes, P Graham (Labour) 548 votes, N Stonehouse (Labour) 538 votes, J Firby (Conservative) 230 votes, J Milner (Conservative) 200 votes. And that was that. All over after twenty one years. Wounds to lick. Time to move on.

Notification offering me early retirement from Mail came a few days after the election. I had worked there for thirty four years and, having paid in additional pensionable contributions since the early days, the offer to voluntarily retire came with a sizeable lump sum and a forty year pension. All I had to do was sign to accept it and I would be free to go with outstanding leave taken into account, on Friday 1st August, two days before my fifty fifth birthday. I signed.

Shortly after signing I went to Liverpool for what would be my last CWU conference. It was a bitter sweet swansong having attended all but five conferences throughout my career. Within the Darlington delegation was my eventual successor Brett Giroux. In his role as the area processing representative, Brett was highly regarded by myself and by employees and managers alike. And as I had grown increasingly restless and tired, devoid of much further interest, I had already singled him out as the man to take over from me as branch secretary. He was young, energetic, bright and knowledgeable; just what the branch needed at the time I was ready for bowing out.

Also in that Liverpool delegation were branch chairman Alan Robson, Legal & Medical Secretary Malcolm Preston, Health & Safety Officer Ian Stevenson and Northallerton Workplace Representative Dave Peers.

Whenever Darlington conference delegates were facing retirement I would organise farewell presentations for them often with notable guest speakers. It was customary too, on the final day of conference, for our national chairman or chairwoman to announce the names of delegates who were attending for the last time. Some, having been duly nominated by their respective branches, were presented with awards, badges and certificates for long or meritorious service. It was all a respectful part of being a member of our vast trade union family.

Imagine my disappointment then when on that closing Friday morning session, there were no delegates from Darlington in the hall save for Dave Peers and myself. I phoned our branch chairman, Alan Robson.

"Hey, Alan. Where are you?"

"On the train. Just pulling in to York, mate."

"What? What the hell are you doing there? Where's everybody else?"

"They're here on the train. We decided to get away early as there's never much going on in the last session. You and Peersie can handle what's left to do."

I couldn't believe it. Here I was, my final day as a conference delegate – *ever* – and apart from Dave Peers none of my branch colleagues, whom I worked with every day, were present for me. Dave was astonished, angry and disappointed for me. I thanked him for his understanding. To cap it all, my name was not read out in the list of honoured delegates attending for their last time. A number of colleagues from around the country came to where I was seated and expressed their surprise; some were embarrassed for me having been what they each saw as let down by my own branch. It was all very comradely but I didn't want a fuss and I kept my feelings in check. But I mean... can you fucking believe it? To be a little fair, though, I had recently stated that I didn't want a fuss by way of a celebration back in Darlington. But nobody from my branch had considered my final conference after thirty four years as being worthy of official note.

When Mike Findley phoned me at home a few weeks later, he told me that he had been surprised to learn that my years of service had not been acknowledged. Mike was a true friend and I thanked him for his concern but that I wished to put the matter behind me. He insisted that he considered the situation unacceptable and that he would write to CWU headquarters highlighting my roles and positions in the union and the wider political movement. In advising headquarters of my service on behalf of local members and the national union, he said he would also request that consideration be given to my being presented with a long service award and badge. I asked him not to but he wouldn't hear of it.

Headquarters response was to remind Mike that it was a matter for individual branches to determine and for them to submit a request for recognition if they felt it was warranted. Without a request from the branch, they advised, my roles, positions and achievements could not be officially acknowledged. Mike and I agreed to forget the whole affair.

Do I harbour a grudge? Nah. Not much. I did at the time but what's done is done and I remain a card carrying retired member. Bless them all.

There was a similar unedifying situation on my final day at work. Sorting mail, as I had done so often alongside Dean O'Neill and fifty or sixty or so others, I was looking forward to finishing my final shift at half past eight. There wasn't much sorting left to do by quarter past eight so I shook Dean's hand and told him I was going home. The shift manager on duty that evening was Mick Howell and I called into his office on the way out.

"Right, Mick. It's just about done out there and as it's my last day I'm heading off now."

"Aye. Okay. See you."

And with that briefest of exchanges I walked through the bustling Mail Centre, out into the corridor leading to the car park and stepped into the light summer evening air. The heavy glass doors closed behind me I turned and looked back. There was nobody there to see me off. Just my reflection in the glass. After all those years!

Janet, Daniel & Padraic, greeted me home with a wonderful wine and champagne buffet. In the warm embrace of that joyous moment, I kissed their kind and loving faces and at once my feelings of 'bollocks to them all' evaporated.

A couple of weeks later I received in the post a fifty pound gift card, redeemable at George in ASDA. It was enclosed with a lovely card signed by a group of about twenty full and part time women colleagues who, they said, had only just found out I had left.

Over the course of the next few weeks Janet and I discussed what I should do next. We had three options: 1. Get another full time job. 2. Find some part time work. 3. Set up FILMAR Photography as a sole trader business.

In the end Janet surprised me with a fourth option.

"Look, Phil", she said. "You've spent all your working life dealing with other peoples issues and concerns. Why not take six months out and do absolutely nothing?"

"Are you serious?"

"Yes. We have enough to live on. Take six months and we'll look at it again next March."

And so I did. Apart from photographing weddings, family portraits and football matches, I also indulged in hill walking, taking solo trips to the coast and countryside, learning new songs, writing and rehearsing with the band, Man With The Stick. I bought and sold guitars and all manner of stringed instruments slowly working them in to a diverse range of songs. There weren't many gigs around this time but those few that I did play were enjoyable enough. Occasionally David Pratt and I would go out as an acoustic duo under the name Out On A Limb and in tandem with the music Janet and I spent a lot of time with David and his partner, Chrissy Heseltine. As a foursome we walked the hills of the North Yorkshire and The Lake District, we sailed in David's boat moored at Pooley Bridge on Ullswater and generally had a jolly good social time together. Our families became close.

Then in March 2009 Janet and I revisited our options. We concluded that I should turn my photographic hobby into a business. I already had the equipment, amassed over many years, so there was no expense there. I built a website, had some cards and leaflets printed and sought advice from a number of business advisors. Before long I was ready to start. Adverts were drawn up and placed in local and regional newspapers; an exercise which cost a bloody fortune and yielded little. Having learned that expensive lesson I set up a Facebook page and began promoting my services on there allowing my business website to act as a 'shop window'. I quickly discovered that social media was far more effective for me than paper advertising.

Business was nevertheless slow at first and I was reminded that it takes on average three years to become established…or fail. I had FILMAR Photography – affordable photographic services – www.filmar.co.uk - emblazoned in gold lettering across the rear of my car giving me additional free advertising wherever I went.

One late summer evening I took a call from Caroline Turrell inviting me to a meeting of local business owners. Caroline was an agent for Utility Warehouse Club and had seen my car advertisement on many occasions. She explained that she was a member of Business Networking International (BNI) whose local chapter met for breakfast once a week in Park Head Hotel; handily right next door to where I lived.

"We are looking for a photographer to refer business to. Would you like to be my guest at an open day we're having soon? There'll be lots of other businesses there who'll be looking forward to meeting you."

I went along and 'got' the BNI "Giver's Gain" philosophy straight away... *if I give you business, you will want to give me business* – and I applied to join. With my application duly approved and only one business from each sector permitted to join, I was the only photographer at the weekly meetings along with just one plumber, one accountant, one architect, one builder, one financial advisor, one solicitor, one florist, one web designer, one graphic designer, one utilities company, one roofer, one electrician, etc, referring business between ourselves and acting as an unpaid sales team for each other.

There are BNI chapters all over the world each generating thousands, sometimes millions of pounds worth of business amongst themselves. Individual member's competitors are effectively locked out meaning that when a colleague in my chapter heard of someone requiring a photographer, they would recommend and refer that business to me. In turn, if I heard of someone needing a plumber or whatever, I recommended and referred likewise. The return on my initial investment – the cost of joining and a small weekly fee to pay for the room and breakfast - was repaid in no time at all. Directly as result of being a member of BNI I saw a forty percent growth in business in my first year alone. By the middle of my second year FILMAR Photography had become well known with commissions for weddings, family portraits, baptisms, sports events, corporate and business shoots and the like continuing to grow. I went on, within three years, to become a BNI Chapter Director and a Regional Executive Director to boot. My turnover and annual net profit grew and grew and many's the time I wished I'd heard of BNI years earlier.

Politics and community affairs were never far away and in May 2009 I was invited to receive the award of Honorary Alderman at the county council's annual meeting. Following a recent review of local government, the county's eight district councils became one and a mighty County Durham Council was established. It was decided to mark the occasion by bestowing the title of honorary alderman on a fair few retired and defeated councillors who had served the previous administration for twenty years or more. Although the title does not convey status in any political or representative capacity it is, nevertheless, one which I am proud to hold.

12 – Guillain Barre Syndrome

The morning of Tuesday 8th October 2013 started out like any other. Janet had left for work by the time I woke up and after showering and dressing, I made my way along the landing and into the room from which I ran FILMAR Photography. In here was a range of electric and acoustic guitars, an Irish bouzouki, mandolin, ukulele, violin and other music accoutrement. My life as a professional musician lived side by side with my photography business. With the laptop booting wearily to life I made coffee and morning emails and see what was happening across the various social media platforms. With no client meetings to attend I relaxed into the cool black leather of my chair and replied to emails, wrote paper notes of phone calls to be made and deleted spam and other irrelevances.

By now it was almost 9am and, with arms aloft, stretching to shake off the stiffness of sleep, I strained a little too far and felt a slight but sharp discomfort in my neck. Ignoring it, like any still active and reasonably fit sixty year old man might do, my eyes and mind turned instead to the pastoral scene outside. I gazed upon the autumn fields soundlessly fallow, the lane leading up to the villages of Coundon and Leeholme, car and people free, the sky overcast was yet bright with weak shadows cast by the now steadily rising invisible sun. It was from this agreeable daily office vantage that I observed the passing of the seasons and the coming and going of wildlife and local industry. Farming activity, in the main. Cattle and sheep, ploughing and harvesting. From here, in late spring, I welcomed the arrival of swallows at the end of their six thousand mile flight from the sweltering heat of southern Africa. Gone now. Back to overwinter from whence they had flown a few warm months before. Life was good. The day ahead promised no drama. I was happy and content with my life, my music and my business.

Picking up one of the Nikon cameras I'd been using the previous weekend I switched the power button to ON. The memory card was half filled with images to download and edit for clients. When placing the camera down on the desk I thought it felt a little heavier than usual. I picked it up. I put it back down. Nah! It felt alright. Or so I surmised. I took a drink of coffee and the cup felt heavy. How strange! I then became aware of an ever so slight tingling down my right arm.

"Ah! I know what this is."

Ten years earlier I had been diagnosed with spondolosis of the fifth and sixth vertebrae near the top of my spine. The treatment I'd had had been successful but I remember being told there was always a chance that the problem might return. It was this, I judged, that was causing the discomfort in my neck and, consequently, the tingling down my arm. I'd see how things went and if there was no improvement in a day or so, I'd make an appointment to have it checked out. By early afternoon, picking up everyday items such as my pen and mobile phone proved tricky. I found myself regularly mistyping and concentrating on where my fingers fell across the keyboard instead of keeping an eye on the screen. Work was slow. For lunch I made sandwiches of tuna and sweetcorn and here, the simple act of opening tins and prising off the lid of the mayonnaise jar proved awkward. I needed to use more strength than usual to manage even these familiar tasks. The tingling in my arm was pretty much the same as earlier but now my fingers and thumbs, although normal to look at, felt swollen and clumsy.

Yet, in spite of what was happening, convinced it was a recurrence of the spondolosis, I was not unduly concerned. I'd already made a mental note to contact my GP if things did not improve and I said nothing about it to Janet when she came home. We spent a typical evening together chatting about work, family, life in general and, after dinner, we shared a bottle of merlot and settled down in front of the tv. Janet, prodigious knitter, click, click, clicked with needles and wool while I variously flicked through news and documentary channels. My hand trembled slightly when taking a sip of wine and I spilled a little on to my shirt. I joked about being pre-drink drunk.

I slept fine but woke next morning to find the tingling had spread to my left arm and to both thumbs and forefingers. I'd make that GP appointment after breakfast. Of course, I never did. I've often heard it said that men are less likely than women to seek medical help and I suppose I add credence to the stereotype. After all, having already been successfully and painlessly treated for spondolosis, I had no need to worry. After ablutions and breakfast I went into my office. What worries I had decreased throughout the day and the symptoms did not appear to be getting worse. My focus, instead, was on finalising arrangements for the coming Saturday's photoshoot.

County Durham Council had commissioned me to photograph the public unveiling of a statue in commemoration of West Auckland Football Club winning the first ever World Cup tournament in 1909. In actual fact the contest had been the forerunner of the Inter City Fairs Cup but time and journalistic license have cemented its modern day mantle into twentieth first century thinking and thus its upgraded reverence in footballing circles and beyond.

Having later finished work and with my mind no longer focused on photography, I decided to tell Janet about the symptoms I was experiencing. As with myself, remembering the past episode with spondolosis, she made no fuss. We ate, we chatted, we lounged and we went to bed. I slept soundly.

Upon waking the following morning and stepping out of bed, I noticed the first sign of weakness in my legs. Stumbling slightly as I stood, I placed one hand on the wall to steady myself while pulling on a dressing gown. I walked awkwardly to the top of the stairs adopting the gait of a man wearing frogman's flippers. Going downstairs I was unsteady and I had to brace myself using the banister with my right hand and with my left on the opposite wall. This was becoming serious.

Awkwardness became the theme of preparing breakfast. It was to be a simple enough meal... cornflakes and coffee. Simple as it was, however, cornflakes and milk were spilled on the worktop and I decided against making coffee. I walked/waddled from the kitchen and sat on the settee in the living room to eat. By now my hands were really weak and I could barely grip the spoon. As I stood up, slowly and awkwardly, I spilled a little residual milk on the carpet. I fetched a kitchen cloth to clean it up and got down on my knees. And that's when the fun began. I couldn't get back up off the floor. My legs were so weak that, after several attempts, I resorted to heaving myself up using my hands and elbows against an arm of the settee.

I telephoned the Health Centre in Coundon and made an appointment to see my GP. Thankfully, I had called early enough to be seen that morning. Making a fist of teeth cleaning I decided to forego the usual morning shower. It took some time to dress properly even though I chose casual pull-on stuff such as trackies, t-shirt, socks and trainers. Surprisingly, driving felt normal and I managed the controls without difficulty. Steering and parking at the Health Centre was a breeze. Stepping out of the car and into the reception was not. Pauline, the receptionist, smiled as she registered me in and bade me take a seat. I selected one with arms.

Dr.Poonah Nair, professionally attractive in a black trouser suit with red buttoned up blouse, around which hung an obligatory stethoscope, smiled as I entered and welcomed me to take a seat. She didn't fail to notice my awkward gait and stood to offer me a helping hand. Once seated I began by explaining my symptoms and answering the usual exploratory questions;

"When did it start?"

"Where did it start?"

"Has it happened before?"

All the while she expertly felt and manipulated my hands, arms, legs and my now sock and trainer-free feet. My blood pressure and temperature were noted and recorded but not before I was asked to commit to memory an address which she read out. After the cuff and thermometer had been set aside she asked me to repeat the address. I did. She smiled. I was then asked if I'd mind dropping my pants and lying down on the examination couch. I was hardly likely to object and did as I was advised. Dr.Nair manoeuvred me onto my left side to face a wall and I felt her gently massaging my feet slowly moving further up past my ankle and calves. I struggled not to squirm from the occasional tickle as she did whatever she had to. The next thing I knew she parted my bum cheeks slightly and proceeded to poke around my anus with what, to me, felt like a sharp stick. With a thank you and an exhortation to get dressed, she washed her hands, moved across to her desk and began making notes on her laptop.

"Philip", my birth name, she said when I had sat down. "I want you to have an MRI scan and you will receive an appointment in the next day or two."

Typically and naturally, I suppose, my own enquiry about what she thought the problem was went unheeded so I merely presumed the scan was to redetermine the extent of the spondolosis. I thanked her. She smiled a silent goodbye and I waddled back down the corridor.

Although weak, I resolved to carry on as near normal as I could. I attended my regular BNI meeting, explaining to astonished colleagues that I was fine,
that my spondolosis was affecting the way I walked and that, following the anticipated scan, I'd soon be as right as rain.

The following morning, Saturday, the sky was overcast and grey and a strengthening cold wind, persistent now, had driven in overnight. These were not the best conditions for photography. Helpfully, the wind eased a little by lunchtime.

My camera bag, not unduly heavy, contained two Nikon bodies, wide angle and standard lenses, flash gun and memory cards. Thus, besuited and mentally prepared, if not physically, I drove to The Manor House Hotel in West Auckland some five miles away for my two o'clock assignment.

A number of dignitaries had already arrived and were drinking tea or coffee and doing not much else other than milling around chatting. In the midst of the hubbub I recognised Derek Foster, former Member of Parliament for Bishop Auckland, now sadly deceased but then Lord Foster of Auckland, Helen Goodman the incumbent MP, Sir John Hall of Metro Centre and Newcastle Football Club fame, The Lord Lieutenant of Durham, Sue Snowden and a stockily built, grandly spoken gent by the name of John Wotherspoon, commercial director of Lipton Teas.

I chatted with one or two people who I recognised whilst others, mainly business leaders, county and local councillors and civic officials, arrived and filled up the ever decreasing space. There were more suits and ties in that steadily burgeoning lounge bar than in Burton's... or Matalan. The ladies, casually eyeing each other's nails, hair and shoes, were resplendent in their finest, if inappropriate for the weather, frocks, coats, hats and fascinators. Nobody mentioned my awkward attempts to walk and stand normally as I photographed the social exchanges before me ahead of the unveiling.

The walk to the statue, a mere one hundred yards or so from the hotel, was slow for me and the muscles in my back ached from the strain of trying to walk normally. By now it had started raining. Those who'd had the forethought to bring umbrellas duly opened them while groups of others huddled closely together to form a shield from the rain and the cold wind. It was a sizeable crowd and I wondered how many actually understood the historical significance of the event which lay ahead. Television crews from ITN and BBC, all Berghaus jackets and hooded microphones, were establishing their pitch setting up heavy, camera mounted, tripods.

The hotel had emptied of its distinguished guests by this time, and they had similarly made their way to the village green. Like the crowd who greeted them, they huddled under their own umbrellas while trying to maintain a look of unperturbed dignity. We got the call that there was to be a delay. Someone from a tv company wished to retime the filming of the event due to other newsworthy developments in the region. Nobody knew quite what but amidst the groans, sighs and a few derisory chortles, the party of dignitaries and other invited sorts, made their sombre, rain soaked way back to the warmth of the hotel lounge. I really struggled now. I gave up trying to keep up and, once inside, found a seat in reception on which to sit. My Nikons were reasonably watertight but, nevertheless, I thought it best to check and dry the one I'd been using thus far and examine the images I'd taken. Everything was fine but by god it felt heavy. Gathering up my camera bag, I made my awkward way to the lounge to rejoin the dampened throng.

When the call came to leave again I was taken by surprise, having planned to be back at the site of the statue to capture shots of my fellow participants arriving. As it turned out, and not unnaturally, they beat me easily. By the time I got there, rain soaked and out of breath, a car conveying the actor and special guest, Tim Healey, pulled up. In that moment an excited fan base of all ages, predominantly women, rushed the car.

The police, try as they might but totally flummoxed, were incapable of holding them back. A hundred or so female soap viewers, all eagerly determined to get close to their cross dressing Benidorm tv hero, and probably with no regard for his epic performance in A Captain's Tale and the celebration of the days commemoration, were too much for two police officers to deal with. Yet somehow, deploying more brute force than charm, my fellow photographers and journalists managed to create an avenue of sorts down which our esteemed tv personality walked straight towards my waiting lens. Gotcha!

The rain had eased to a pour in time for the plaque unveiling. Speeches were mercifully short but delivered by more speakers than was necessary. The crowd remained in good spirits throughout and I managed to get the shots I needed.

The constant struggle to preserve my balance, with back muscles screaming with pain and fearful for my wet gear, was taking its toll on my concentration. I needed a break. With space and time to spare, I knelt down to take some final shots of the polished bronze plaque, shooting low to capture the statue figures against the gloomy sky. It was not a wise decision. I could not get back up. Thankfully, Andy Lamb, a photographer from The Northern Echo, taking similar shots, saw my predicament and helped me to my feet. Somewhat embarrassed, I thanked him and with a quick explanation, bade farewell and waddled, much more slowly now, to present myself at the drinks reception and grand dinner.

Janet looked at me aghast when I walked in the house that evening. Bedraggled and knackered beyond belief I took a difficult shower, pulled on some warm casual clothes and laid down on the settee, exhausted and in pain.

Of course, in the light of a new day, matters assumed a different perspective. Sunday was drier and brighter and I went through the now familiar motions of struggling to get up, wash, clean my teeth and get dressed. The pain in my back had gone but my arms and legs remained weak. Over breakfast Janet, alert now to what was going on, questioned me in some detail. This was the first time I had considered the possibility that what I was experiencing might have nothing to do with spondolosis.

When the appointment letter regarding the scan did not arrive in Monday's mail my mood changed at once. Down! By then I was a lot weaker and increasingly concerned. I had foolishly scoured the internet and was now convinced I was in the early stages of Motor Neurone Disease. Again, I chose not to share my thoughts with Janet. Instead I telephoned the Health Centre.

Dr.Nair wanted me to go straight to her surgery. I wasted no time bar difficulty with walking to the car and driving to the Health Centre. As soon as I arrived I was ushered straight in to Dr.Nair's room. She took one look at me, her face now showing concern, bade me sit down and picked up the phone. I listened with growing interest to the one sided conversation taking place in front of me.

"This patient of mine is very sick!"

"He must be admitted today!"

"No, no, no. It can't wait. I am being very serious!"

"I am sorry but this man needs seeing today!"

Her insistence to whoever it was on the other end of the phone, paid off. I was to go home, contact Janet and go immediately to James Cook University Hospital in Middlesbrough.

Even then, in the unfamiliar surroundings of a waiting room in the hospital, I resolved to be strong; for Janet, mainly. When a porter arrived with a trolley to take me to the scan, I refused it and elected to walk. I wished I hadn't. The hospital is vast and the walk was long. My legs and back ached. Janet was imploring me not to be "so bloody stupid." She was right. I was being stupid. I stopped being stupid when the scan process was explained to me. I confirmed that I wasn't, to the best of my knowledge, claustrophobic, another bald lie and, that yes, I'd be okay and that I would definitely press the hand held alarm if it all became too much to bear.

All we had to do now was sit and wait for the result. When it came it was conclusive only in the sense that it confirmed that the problem was not spondolosis. There was nothing of concern to show and I was advised to go back to my GP.

Assuming, with today's technology, that hospitals and doctor surgeries liaise over the internet, and that, therefore, my scan results from the day before would be on file in the Health Centre, I telephoned to discuss the result. Dr.Nair wasn't in.

"She won't be in at all today," said Pauline.

And so, Wednesday drew itself inexorably out in an air of uncertainty bordering on fear. My arms and legs were now so weak that I could barely raise a cup or walk to the kitchen. Thankfully we have a downstairs bathroom and toilet and I was capable, with care and concentration, of stumbling to and fro holding on to furniture and kitchen worktops. The only stumbling block, and I say this glibly in light of all the other stuff going on, was that once on the toilet, I had difficulty getting back off. In addition, and readers with sensitivity to matters anatomical are advised to steel themselves as feeling in my penis had all but disappeared.

This had a number of implications, as you might imagine, but for now we'll leave things with the following... inadvertently peeing on the floor became a particular embarrassment! None more so, when having elected to sleep on the settee instead of negotiating the increasingly difficult stairs, I needed the toilet through the night. Struggling to get off the settee I made my feeble way to the bathroom, did what I had to do and then...buggar! Thinking I had finished peeing, I stepped back to see myself now peeing on to the floor. Remembering my earlier difficulty cleaning up spilled milk, I was going to be extremely cautious cleaning up this particular mess. Caution mattered not. I was unable to stand up afterwards.

Try as I might I could not raise myself from the bathroom floor. I didn't have strength, even, to lift myself by my arms and the bathroom sink. I called out for Janet. I called out several times. Just more futility. With the particular configuration of downstairs bathroom to upstairs bedroom, solid walls, closed doors and Janet away in dreamsleep, it would be hard for her to hear the eruption of Krakatoa, let alone the plaintive cry of her increasingly debilitated husband. I gave up calling and crawled, slowly and painfully on hands and knees, back to the settee, it in itself a major obstacle to climb.

It was now ten days since the first, imperceptible, signs of whatever it was that was occurring, and I was now virtually immobile. When Janet came downstairs and listened to me relating what happened through the night, she was mortified. We agreed that we had to push for more to be done. But what? The only available option at the time was, yet again, to try to get Dr.Nair on the phone.

Once with Dr.Nair I was put through similar tests to those which she had conducted the previous week, including the sharp pointed stick to the bum. She was appalled to learn from me that the MRI scan had concluded only that I didn't have spondolosis. I knew my situation was serious when she raised her eyes to the ceiling and loudly exclaimed,

"Good grief! Did they not do a brain scan?"

Now, that unexpected outburst shook me like never before. Could this be the turning point? The good doctor made an extremely insistent phone call. I guessed, by now, that she was good at this. Somebody was getting the mother of all ear bashings. I loved her for it. The upshot was that

Janet was now to drive me straight to hospital, tout suite and no stopping on the way. Little did we know that our lives were about to change irrevocably and that it would be nearly ten months before I would see our home again.

13 – The Final Chapter

I was discharged from hospital on August 1st 2014, just two days before my 61st birthday and two weeks prior to Daniel's wedding to Emma Sams. Padraic was the best man and I was so proud of my lovely family and in laws and a host of other relatives and friends. Perfect.

I had been admitted to hospital the previous October with Guillain Barre Syndrome (GBS). It's a very rare illness with only around a thousand or so affected each year in the UK. Some eighty percent of people go on to make a full recovery, the rest, as with myself, live with what is referred to as residual damage and a few, thankfully very few, die.

Confined to a wheelchair and having to learn how to walk unaided I was dependent upon others for mobility. Janet had our bed moved downstairs and with the wheelchair and a zimmer frame I was able, with care, to get to and from our downstairs bathroom and toilet. A bathchair enabled me to shower and a toilet frame and riser were handy as well. Claire & Tony Gibbons, owners of Park Head Hotel where Janet works as duty manager, generously and kindly gave her time off as necessary to tend to my needs during recovery.

In time and after many weeks of outpatient physiotherapy in Bishop Auckland General Hospital and with invaluable help from Richard Crawford, a personal trainer in the gym at Woodhouse Close Leisure Complex, I gained sufficient strength to walk slowly with crutches. In turn the crutches yielded to a pair of walking sticks.

And that's pretty much where I am today hurtling inexorably towards my older age. I have limited feeling with weakness in my hands, legs and feet and I endure fatigue on a regular basis having to rest frequently. All this means I need to be extremely careful when walking out and about. And although discharged from further NHS consultations unless I feel I need to return, I take a daily plethora of tablets for all manner of deficiencies while low level post traumatic stress and depression remain a constant feature. And things are unlikely to improve. Scottish comedian and actor, Billy Connolly, who also has a neuropathy illness, Parkinson's disease, once said, and I paraphrase, 'Every illness I have ever had in my life always went away. Parkinson's won't go away.' Which, ironically for me, is fine when I recall being paralysed from the neck down for most of the ten months I was in hospital and where, on one occasion, I came close to dying.

During my time in hospital Janet and the wives of two fellow GBS patients, Ken Longstaff and Barry Singh, heard about a charity specifically for Guillain Barre Syndrome. Based in Sleaford, Lincolnshire, Guillain Barre & Associated Inflammatory Neuropathies, or GAIN to save a mouthful, campaigns to highlight awareness and understanding of the illness and to raise vital funds for research. There is a website – www.gaincharity.co.uk – with lots of helpful information and resource for patients and academics. Janet, Beverley Longstaff and Val Singh contacted GAIN and arranged for one of their people, Gill Ellis, to come to the hospital and meet with us to explain what the charity does, how it helps and to answer questions which we had.

We learned a lot from Gill and after I was discharged I considered responding to a vacancy request to become a Trustee of the charity. I met the then chairman James Babbington-Smith over lunch in Darlington with the charity's director, Caroline Morrice, and was sufficiently intrigued to submit an application. Sadly, during a later meeting with interview in Peterborough, it quickly became apparent that my diary as a singer in a band – something that Guillain Barre had not taken away - prevented me from ever being available to the Trustees. Instead I volunteered to be one of a handful of supporters willing to speak over the telephone with patients and their families to try and give some semblance of comfort that, although alarming and debilitating, GBS is recoverable in the vast majority of cases. The phone calls made me acutely aware of the disparities in the treatment received depending on where one lived in the UK. With GBS being so rare there is very little experience of

237

it in the wider NHS and only a few GP's have ever come across it in their surgeries. As a result it is often difficult to diagnose and many people are initially misdiagnosed.

Obviously, I couldn't speak as a medical professional but relaying my personal experience gave people and their families some perspective and hope. The biggest problem for me, however, was that the calls were often highly emotional with each one bringing back vivid memories of what I had been through. I was mentally bruised for hours after. What I didn't realise was that my emotional and mental post-call recovery was getting longer and longer as the months passed. It got to the point where I began to dread call requests coming through from GAIN and following a particularly tearful call from a woman in Essex, I broke down and wept uncontrollably. I was in a dreadful state for days afterwards and I began to realise that the phone calls were wreaking havoc on me. In January 2019 I could take no more and, with sadness I withdrew from the support service. Even that action left me feeling guilty and ashamed.

With my life having changed and unable to even hold a camera, let alone take pictures, I sold my photography business in 2015. Hill walking, cycling and tennis were no longer accessible to me and being helpful around the house became nigh on impossible. The band I was in at the time, prophetically called Man With The Stick, had changed too because I could no longer play my instruments. We advertised for a replacement guitarist while I confined myself to singing from a performer's stool. It didn't work. The dynamics had changed, differences of opinion arose and I was unhappy with the lack of progress towards live playing. I left in March 2015.

I now had nothing apart from my family and GBS. I was miserable and inconsolable and found myself withdrawn and prone to angry outbursts. It was a dark, sombre and self pitying period after a lifetime of active pursuits and personal achievement. Nevertheless, from the darkness of that time a light began to shine. I called two of my friends, Geoff Pickering and Bill Oxbrough, and asked them to meet me to discuss an idea I had for a new musical project. I asked them what they thought about setting up an electro-acoustic trio with them playing guitars and myself simply singing. Explaining that there would be no need for a large PA and that shows could be set up and dismantled with ease, I said I'd just need to rely on them for transport. They both liked the idea and in May 2015 Share The Darkness was launched.

At the time we were not an Irish band. We played country and soft rock mainly along the likes of Gram Parsons, The Saw Doctors and Lindisfarne until one night in O'Connell's in Middlesbrough we were approached during the interval by music and events promoter, Angie Taylor.

"You should consider turning Irish", she said.

Now, I have always enjoyed performing Irish songs but I have to admit to never having considered a fully Irish act.

"Have you not noticed that every time you play an Irish song there's a different reaction from the audience?"

"Can't say we've taken much notice", I replied.

"Well, think about it. There aren't many bands in the north east who do totally Irish and you guys would be very good at it."

During our second set I listened and observed and, sure enough, she was right. There was indeed a much better response to our Irish stuff and we left that night to start rehearsing an all Irish set which we completed in a matter of weeks. It was a fortuitous move and by November 2016 we had grown a healthy fanbase and were nominated as "Best Traditional Act ~ 2016" in the Ubeat TV Awards with Tyne & Wear, Sky and Living TV. It was a heady awards ceremony and Janet and I went with Geoff Pickering and his wife, Chris, and our fiddle player, Willem A. De Bruijne, to a glitzy ceremony in the O2 Academy in Newcastle upon Tyne. We didn't win the award but were happy to have been beaten by Toni Sidgewick, a superb songstress from Shetland.

We'd had a few changes of personnel by the time of the nomination with Bill leaving to pursue his career with Groundwork North East, Mark Hammonds joining us on

240

guitar, Jim Robinson came in on stick bass and Willem A. De Bruijne on fiddle. Jim had then left and was replaced by Gary Lee. Now we were forging ahead with bookings galore and a growing fanbase of friends and followers. But then, in May 2017, with a diary filled with summer and autumn bookings, Willem left to return to his family in Dusseldorf.

Fiddle players, good ones I mean, are extremely rare in the north east and those that can play well are committed elsewhere. We interviewed, auditioned and rejected three or four eventually giving the role to Maddy Sutcliffe who introduced herself at one of our shows in Spennymoor's The Frog & Ferret. Sadly, things didn't work out and after a few months of patience, coupled with an element of frustration as she tried valiantly to get to grips with what we required, both Maddy and we parted company.

Welcome Cathy Edmunds. Cathy has played in orchestras, is a teacher, writer, poet, artist and one of the finest fiddle players I have ever had the good fortune to know. She is admired wherever we play.

And so the line up today in Share The Darkness – more Irish than a Dublin pub – is Geoff Pickering, Mark Hammonds, Gary Lee, Cathy Edmunds and yours truly. A veritable tour de force and the best band I have ever been in.

We are almost at the end now so stay with me just a little bit longer. Thank you for your forbearance thus far.

A life in Labour Party politics, the trade union movement, music and photography will not appeal to everyone. Indeed, as I stated in the Notes & Explanation, interest in my particular life will be limited to a few who may be similarly inclined or who have been mentioned within these pages. To me, though, it has been a life of fulfilment and pleasure. I feel privileged in so many ways and if I were to be granted my time over again there is little that I would do differently.

Apologies, of sorts, to anyone who I may have namedropped and who might feel affronted by what I have written. Tough. That's how it seemed to me at the time. And, conversely, to anyone who I have not namedropped and who feel they should have been included, apologies, too. There are so many good and valued people whose lives have crossed my own and there simply isn't time nor space to do justice to you all.

I live with the aftermath and consequences of Guillain Barre Syndrome which I always said should not define me. Unfortunately, it has and it is endured daily. I can not change its insidious effect but I try, mostly successfully, to get along with the blessed thing and enjoy all that I can still do. Above all, my life is blessed with a loving and supportive family, superb musicians in Share The Darkness, many wonderful people I count as friends and from having had experiences only a few are fortunate to know.

Lightning Source UK Ltd.
Milton Keynes UK
UKHW012110210222
399015UK00001B/28

9 781839 458040